CULTURE by DESIGN

8 simple steps to drive better individual and organizational performance

David J. Friedman

ISBN 978-0-692-10078-3 paperback
ISBN 978-1-49-583050-1 hardcover
ISBN 978-1-49-583052-5 eBook

Printed in the United States of America

HIGH PERFORMING
CULTURE, LLC
www.HighPerformingCulture.com
877-HPC-5050

CONTENTS

Introduction

I live in a small town in southern New Jersey, just across the Delaware River from Philadelphia, called Moorestown. It's an idyllic community of roughly 20,000 residents, founded by Quakers in 1682, with tree-lined streets, a quaint downtown Main Street, and one public high school. While Moorestown High School is known for the high academic achievement of its students, it's also known for one particular sport: girls' lacrosse. For as many years as I can remember, the girls' lacrosse team has been dominating the region, and they can frequently be seen ranked in the top ten nationally. In fact, in the 16 seasons from 2000 to 2015, the girls' lacrosse team won the state championship an astonishing 15 times.

Less than 15 miles from Moorestown is another suburban town that's known as Voorhees Township. The public high school in Voorhees is called Eastern Regional High School. More than any other sport, Eastern is renowned for its girls' field hockey program. Over the past two decades, the Eastern field hockey team has won 18 consecutive state championships, during which they also put together a national record 153-game unbeaten streak.

Not 25 miles from Voorhees is yet another small southern NJ town with a fascinating story. Paulsboro is what you might call a working-class town. It has roughly 6,000 residents, and one public high school. Beyond anything else, Paulsboro High

School is famous for its wrestling program. In fact, from 1983 to 2008, the wrestling team won 25 consecutive state championships. Over a nearly 40-year period, they won an amazing 307 consecutive conference matches.

While these three schools are all in southern NJ, there are countless similar examples in virtually every state across the country. No doubt you can name some in the area where you live.

Two factors

I find public high school sports dynasties to be particularly fascinating because they have two dynamics that make them rather unique. First, as public schools, for the most part, they can't recruit. In other words, they're largely stuck with whoever coincidentally happens to live in their town. And there's no reason to suggest that Moorestown residents have an inherent talent for lacrosse or that Paulsboro residents are simply born as good wrestlers.

Second, they turn over their rosters at least every four years; and more typically, every year, since most starters are probably seniors. So if these teams can manage to win championships year after year over several decades, when they're limited by who just happens to live there and they're doing it with a different cast of characters each time, there *must be* something special that's creating such a continuous string of success.

Certainly they have great feeder programs for their youth, supportive parents, and without question, they have great coaches. But more than that, they've created championship *cultures*. In fact, a culture of success permeates every aspect of how they operate. They've developed an expectation of success that literally becomes infused in every player who joins the team. They think like champions, they train like champions, and they play like champions. It's simply who they are.

And here's the really interesting thing: If the family of one of those players moves to another town, and the student now attends a different high school and joins a different team, I don't think they play at the same level. The culture of the team significantly influences the player's performance.

Fitting in

You see, it's natural for us, even unconsciously, to want to fit in with our peer group. When those around us are all working hard, trying to achieve at the highest level, and holding each other accountable, most of us will do what's necessary to fit in. And when those around us are less committed, aren't willing to put in the effort, or don't really care, most of us will similarly match the expected level of intensity.

Think back over your life. Have you ever been part of a championship sports team at any level? Or perhaps a great dance troupe, or a high performing band, orchestra, or choral group? Wasn't there a level of expectation in the group that caused you to perform at a higher level than you might have otherwise naturally done? And if you've ever been part of a team that had the opposite culture, didn't that also affect your personal performance and that of your teammates?

The culture of the group truly has that much influence over each individual member's performance. This is as true for a sports team as it is for an orchestra or a business or any other group of people. Simply put, the culture of any group of people has an enormous influence over how each of the people do what they do. And as such, it has an extraordinary impact on the group's overall performance.

Creating culture intentionally

So what's the implication of this recognition of the influence that culture has on performance as it relates to leadership? Well, as a leader, think of the enormous impact you could have if you had some way that you could more purposely or more intentionally create the kind of culture that would help your team to perform at the highest level. Think of how this could affect customer service, recruiting, turnover, sales, profitability; literally every aspect of performance.

But is culture something you can really *create*, or is it simply something that happens organically, haphazardly, based on the people who've coincidentally come together?

The purpose of this book is not only to answer that question (sneak peek: you absolutely *can* and *should* create the culture you want), but more importantly, to show you *how* to do it. More than anything, this is a practical book that will give you a simple roadmap, complete with detailed instructions, for building a truly high-performing culture on your team.

This is also a very personal book, based on my own experience, first as the CEO of an award-winning company with an amazing culture, and then as the founder and CEO of High Performing Culture, LLC and the creator of the Fundamentals System.™

It represents the accumulated learning from my own leadership experience, as well as from that of working with literally hundreds of other organizations and leaders, guiding them through the original process that I created and have since continued to augment.

Let me briefly share that personal story here, as it does provide important context for the concepts and the techniques that follow.

The RSI years

I spent 27 years building and running an employee benefits consulting company called RSI, which we grew from two employees to a staff of well over 100 professionals and annual revenue in excess of $16 million. During the years that I was leading that company, we were many times named one of the Best Places to Work in both NJ and the Philadelphia region, were many times named one of the fastest-growing privately-held companies in the region, and won numerous other awards for service, quality, and leadership. As successful as we were, it might surprise you to learn that the foundation for it all was the culture we had built.

The hallmark of that culture was a series of behaviors that we taught which were known as our Fundamentals. We focused on one of these Fundamentals each week through a series of practices, or rituals. Over time, these Fundamentals became ingrained in our people so that they were practically part of our company's very DNA.

In 2008, we sold RSI to a large, multi-billion-dollar, publicly-held company, after which I spent two years running RSI as a division of this larger entity, before retiring from that industry in 2010.

In 2011, I wrote my first book, *Fundamentally Different*, which many of you may have also read. It was a book largely about the specific culture we had created at RSI and the Fundamentals that made that culture so special and so effective. I've always been very candid about the fact that *Fundamentally Different* was written as a closure step, as a way of wrapping up my old career in a neat package with a nice bow on top, so that, having created appropriate closure to that phase of my career, I would feel free to pursue something entirely new and different. Little did I know that wasn't to happen!

As people read the book and found great value in its lessons, I was asked to speak, mostly to groups of CEOs. And as these CEOs heard me speak, many began to ask if I could help them apply these same lessons in their organizations. Before I knew it, I was traveling across the country giving talks and working with clients in a wide variety of industries.

From a "hobby" to a "business"

I often describe 2012–2014 as my "hobby phase." I was working alone, having fun, adding value for leaders and their organizations, and finding satisfaction in seeing the impact of my ideas. At the time, I had no grander plan than that. In fact, when friends or relatives would ask about my plans for the future, I would often say, quite honestly, that I had none. If I got bored, I'd stop doing it, and if I found something else that seemed interesting, I might go down an entirely new path.

And yet, every time I would talk to another group of CEOs, I'd get the same astonished reaction. They would tell me that despite the many speakers they'd heard talk about culture, this was the first time anyone had ever made culture so clear and practical and actionable and sustainable. They'd say this was truly different and something they could immediately put to use. Having heard this same message over and over again, I began to appreciate that I had indeed created something that was genuinely unique and powerful, and I realized it would be a shame if the world's exposure to this content was limited to me "playing" with it as a hobby.

And so, in late 2014, working with a friend and former marketing executive, Sean Sweeney, we created the company called High Performing Culture, LLC, and began to create a host of products, tools, and resources that today are collectively known as the Fundamentals System™. We also began to hire staff and train other consultants to implement the system.

As of this writing, I've given more than 300 workshops for thousands of CEOs, explaining the concepts and teaching the methodology that you're about to learn. We've implemented this system in more than 200 companies so far, and have seen and heard about the powerful impact it's had in virtually every case. You'll hear some of these stories throughout this book. Many of our clients tell us that it's the single most impactful thing they've done in the history of their company. It's that big, and it's my pleasure to share it with you here.

Before we jump in though, I want to give you two warnings.

There are no secrets

My first warning is a bit of a confession: as big and powerful as this content is, everything I'm about to share with you is so obvious and simple that it's almost stunning. I'm putting that out there for you here and now because you're likely to quickly come to that same realization when you read a section and think to yourself, "Gee, that makes an awful lot of sense" or "That doesn't seem so complicated." And that's the whole point. It *is* simple.

You see, one of my pet peeves is the notion that there are "secrets" out there that only the experts know, with the implication being that if you only knew what they knew, success would easily and magically be yours. Just look at the titles of most business or self-help books. They usually look like this:

- The 3 Secrets to Sales Success
- The 5 Secrets to Being a Great Public Speaker
- The 4 Secrets to Winning Every Negotiation

In stark contrast to the "secrets" myth, my experience is that most of life's most important lessons aren't secrets at all. In fact, virtually anything important that I've ever learned, once I learned it, I literally hit myself in the head and thought, "How did I ever get to be this age and never notice that before?!" I'll bet you've had the same experience. The actual concept wasn't so magical or mysterious; I just hadn't noticed it before. And then, along came a teacher or author or speaker who was able to connect the dots in a way that had previously never occurred to me. For the first time, something clicked, and it now made perfect sense.

My goal is to do the same for you as it relates to culture; to connect the dots for you in a new and simple way. That is, to demystify culture in a way that makes it accessible and easy to understand, and more importantly, easy to implement.

Challenging conventional wisdom

My second warning is that some of the ideas that I'm going to share with you may at first seem to fly in the face of conventional wisdom, or they may seem counterintuitive. They may even conflict with suggestions you've read or heard before. I assure you though, that if you keep an open mind, and allow me to develop the compelling logic behind each concept, you'll start to appreciate just how practical this is and why it works so well.

As a former and current CEO, I care about practicality above anything else. I've found that the mainstream literature on culture, however, is often filled with complex models that seem scholarly and profound, but end up to be pretty difficult to put into action, or they aren't practical enough to be sustainable over the long run. As you'll no doubt begin to appreciate, implemented properly, the Fundamentals System is the opposite of that. It's simple, it's practical, it's sustainable, and it just works.

While I certainly don't want to make the claim that it's the *only* system that can work, I offer it to you as a practical alternative that has a growing history of success. As you read, allow yourself to let go of all that you may have previously heard or read, and evaluate the approach on its own merit. See if it makes as much sense to you as it does to the thousands of other leaders who've been exposed to this content.

With the background set, and those "qualifiers" out of the way, we're now ready to get to work.

The Impact of Culture

Have you noticed that today, more than ever before, culture has become the "hot topic" in business? You can hardly open a business newspaper or magazine without finding some article about the importance of organizational culture. In Deloitte's annual study of human capital trends, culture is consistently ranked among the top three most important issues for senior leadership. And it's not just limited to business. Collegiate and professional sports teams are talking about creating a culture of winning. Universities are talking about creating a culture of tolerance or inclusion. School systems are talking about creating a culture of respect. Interestingly enough, in 2014, the most looked-up word in Merriam Webster's online dictionary was the word "culture."

So what's driving this recent enthusiasm for culture? From a business perspective, the single biggest factor is the commoditization of our economy. Let me show you why these two issues are so closely linked.

Differentiation in a commoditized world

One of the fundamental challenges that every business faces is the need to provide the marketplace with some compelling reason to choose to do business with you rather than your competitors. What separates you from the rest? What makes you different and better than others who are in the same industry? Whether you're a builder or an IT service provider or an electrician, distributor, doctor, or realtor, you're faced with the same basic challenge—finding a way to differentiate yourself.

And yet, as important as this is, it's actually harder today than at any point in our history to truly differentiate yourself. Said another way, it's easier than it's ever been to copy each other. However you describe what makes you unique is posted all over your website, is splashed across every social media platform, and is highlighted in your advertising . . . as it should be. And it's just not that difficult to copy. To make matters worse, whatever amount of time, effort, and money it took you to create that differentiation, it will typically take your competitors a fraction of that to copy it.

The result of this dynamic is a commoditized marketplace, where most businesses or people offer largely the same thing, or at least claim to offer the same thing. And if potential customers can't figure out what makes one product or service different from another, on what basis do they make their buying decision? You guessed it: price! If the products all appear to be the same, I'll just buy the lowest-priced one. This constant downward pressure on pricing naturally depresses profit margins, making it more and more difficult for businesses to survive.

What* vs. *how

So how do some companies manage to compete and thrive year after year in a commoditized environment? Here's the key: they don't win because of *what* they offer; rather, they win because of *how* they go about offering it. It's how their people work together, how they treat customers, and how they interact with vendors and suppliers that sets them apart.

One of my favorite books on this topic is called *Winning Behavior: What the smartest, most successful companies do differently*, by Terry Bacon and David Pugh. According to the research done by the authors, quality products and competitive pricing are the minimum requirements to be in the game. But those are relatively easy to copy. Real and lasting differentiation comes not from the product but from the actual behavior of the employees, or what they call "behavioral differentiation."

To be clear, I'm not suggesting that we shouldn't be innovative and continue to improve our products and services. It's just that these are minimum requirements to be in the game and, at best, they merely create a short-term window of opportunity rather than a lasting competitive advantage.

Last year, I bought a pair of wireless headphones for listening to music while I work out. At the time, being wireless was a fairly new feature that gave some companies a competitive advantage over those who only offered the more traditional, wired headphones. Within months, however, the market was flooded with wireless alternatives, and at lower and lower price points. For a brief window of time, the product differentiation was meaningful, but it certainly wasn't a lasting competitive advantage.

Creating a sustainable competitive advantage

One of my favorite examples of a company that thrives based on the behavior of its people is the Ritz-Carlton hotel chain. People don't go to a Ritz-Carlton because their beds are more comfortable or their rooms are bigger. They go because of the way they're treated. People share legendary stories about amazing experiences they've had when staying at a Ritz-Carlton property.

Here's the thing I find most fascinating, though: Ritz-Carlton teaches classes at their headquarters where anyone can learn their "secrets"—how they manage to get their people to consistently "out-behave" their competitors. Take a moment to consider that. You work for the Hyatt Regency and you can sign up take a course where Ritz-Carlton will reveal the keys to their competitive advantage! How many of us would invite our competitors in and show them everything we're doing? Not many, I'll bet.

So why would Ritz-Carlton be willing to do this? Because their competitive advantage is wrapped up in how their people behave, and that's so deeply embedded in the DNA of their culture, they know that most competitors won't have the commit ment and the discipline to make it happen, *even when they've been given the formula!*

Ritz-Carlton isn't alone in sharing their formula with the public, including competitors. Companies like Disney, Zappos, Zingerman's, and many others have actually created entire businesses around teaching other companies the keys to their success. Sounds pretty crazy, doesn't it?

But here's the important thing: They're not the least bit worried that competitors will be able to pull it off. That's the power of being able to differentiate *by your people.* Not only is it the last remaining opportunity for competitive advantage in a commoditized world, but it's the most *sustainable* competitive advantage you can create, because it's so darn hard to copy. And of course, creating a team of people who all consistently behave in a differentiated way is driven completely by the culture of the organization.

Attracting and retaining talent

Beyond the critical issue of competitive advantage, there are many other financial implications of working on your culture. Think about your ability to attract and retain key talent. As the millennial generation begins to dominate the workforce, we're seeing a significant shift in what's important to them from a workplace. More than any of their predecessors, Millennials want to feel connected to their work. They want to feel a sense of shared purpose. They'll take a job for less money, and stay at a job, if they feel aligned with the organization's culture. That's not to suggest that we should pay them less, of course, but rather it's to suggest that culture is a major factor in the ability to recruit and retain the talent necessary to succeed at a high level. And while this may be especially true for Millennials, it's not lost on people of other generations as well.

The impact on productivity

In the workshops that I conduct, mostly with CEOs, I often ask the participants to rate the average productivity of their workforce on a scale of 1-10, with 1 meaning that most people don't even show up to work, and 10 meaning that most people are producing to their highest capability given their level of talent or skill. When I go around the room, most leaders will rate the average of their people somewhere between about 6 and 8.

Then I ask them to imagine what it would mean if they could somehow move each person up a few notches on the productivity scale. In other words, those who were 5s moved up to 7s and those who were 7s moved up to 9s and so on. If this could somehow happen, the difference would virtually all go straight to the bottom line! After all, you're paying these people the same amount, but they'd now be producing far more at the same cost.

While there are, of course, a variety of factors that influence any given person's level of productivity (as a percentage of what they're capable of producing), I would argue that the culture in which they're operating is the single biggest factor. Remember our discussion of high school sports dynasties in the Introduction? The environment in which we operate has enormous influence over what we do and how we do it. Put people in a high-performing environment and they're far more likely to raise their level of play to match what they see around them. And the opposite is equally true.

Other financial implications of culture

Beyond increasing productivity (getting more done), think about how your culture affects the way your people treat customers and the impact this has on sales and customer retention. I recently bought a pair of shoes online from Zappos. Unfortunately, they were too big, so I needed to return them and order another size. When I called to get some help on the process, every part of the experience was warm, friendly, helpful, and as painless as they could make it. It made me much more likely to want to buy from them again. And none of that was by accident. Zappos is incredibly intentional about creating a culture that generates these types of customer experiences.

How many times have you dealt with a company where the employees just didn't seem to care? Where you got the clear impression they were just "punching a clock" or "following the rules" with little genuine interest in helping you? How does that affect your desire to do business with that company? The culture in the organization affects *every* aspect of the customer interaction.

As you can see, culture affects our ability to differentiate ourselves in a commoditized marketplace, it affects our ability to attract and retain talented workers, it affects how productive those workers are, and it affects every aspect of the customer interaction. Yes, it's *that* important. No wonder everyone's talking about it these days!

But what *is* culture and where does it come from? Let's take a closer look at that next.

How Does Culture Happen?

We all talk about culture, and we have a general sense or notion of what it is, and yet coming up with a clear definition can be pretty elusive. Some will describe culture as the "personality" of an organization, or the "way people interact and relate to each other" or the "shared beliefs, assumptions, and norms for how a group operates."

I once heard someone describe it this way: "After you go through the new employee orientation and you're sitting in the lunchroom with two people who've been there for years, ask them, 'So, what's it *really* like around here?' However they answer that question, that's the real culture."

In my first book, *Fundamentally Different*, I offered this working definition of a group's culture:

> *Culture is the commonly-held set of values and principles that shows up in the everyday behavior of the people.*

The first part of this definition focuses on the fact that it's commonly held. In other words, the culture isn't necessarily what the leader says it is, or what she wishes it were. Rather, it's the way most people in the group actually think, believe, and behave.

The second part of the definition suggests that the culture is rooted in behavior. Regardless of what people say they value or believe, what actually shows up in their behavior is the best indication of the true culture. We've all seen companies with beautiful posters that articulate their "core values," claiming this to be their culture, while the behavior of their team members would suggest that the culture is truly something very different. For me, the culture is best recognized by looking at the actual behavior of the people.

As you'll see, this behavioral orientation to culture is an essential premise of this book and the very foundation of the Fundamentals System you're going to learn.

Every group has a culture

Here's an interesting observation: Every organization has a culture. Whether you're a customer or a new employee, as soon as you walk into a business, or even call a company, you get a feel for what it's like. Are people friendly? Do they smile? Is it neat and organized, or dirty and messy? How do people relate to each other? How do they relate to a stranger? How do they answer the phone? Consciously or unconsciously, you're picking up the vibe of how things happen there.

And the same is true for every other group of people, from a sports team to a country club to a classroom to a group of friends. When people come together, a culture forms.

Think about a group of your friends. Undoubtedly there's a set of norms, largely unwritten, for how the group operates. What's it OK to joke about? What topics, if any, are off limits? How do you treat new members to the group?

I'm a golfer. At the club where I belong, there are lots of different groups of friends, each with their own culture. Some like to play early and some play late. Some welcome others to join them, while others don't. Some like to bet for a lot of money, and some never bet. Some like to tell off-color jokes, and others find that offensive. They each have their unique culture.

How does a culture form?

Obviously, most groups of friends don't come together and draft a vision, mission, and set of core values to govern how they operate. Instead, the culture happens pretty naturally, even accidentally. But how does this take place?

Here's my observation: In every group, there tends to be one or more people who have a stronger personality than others. They're natural leaders. They're the alpha dogs. And by the energy of their personality, they usually have a disproportionate amount of influence over the group norms. They're the ones who typically suggest where to meet for dinner and at what time, or how much to bet on the golf game. And everyone else tends to follow along.

By the way, those with strong personalities aren't necessarily the loudest ones. Some can be quietly influential, but they're influential nonetheless.

When you join the group, or consider joining the group, you're evaluating, even unconsciously, whether the group norms (which largely have been established by the leader) work for you. If they do, you stay with the group and the norms continue to be reinforced over time. And if they don't work for you, you drop out of the group. Again, much of this is unconscious.

There's usually some trial and error that helps to form the culture as well. You tell a joke that makes the group uncomfortable and you quickly learn not to do that if you want to fit in. The point here though, is that the group's norms are being heavily influenced, in a disproportionate way, by those with the strongest personalities.

So how does this relate to business or other more formal organizations?

The same thing happens in companies

Here's the main point I want you to consider: *absent an intentional force on your part*, the exact same thing is happening in your company. In other words, if you're not purposely and intentionally creating the culture you want to have, it's going to be created anyway, mostly influenced by those with the strongest personalities.

And those with the strongest personalities aren't necessarily the designated managers, supervisors, or leaders. They're simply the people with the strongest personalities. If those people happen to be hardworking, quality-oriented, enthusiastic people, everything will likely work out fine. But what if they're not? What if they're sarcastic, cynical, lazy jerks? You guessed it! They're going to influence those around them to be more like them. I'm sure you've seen this many times. They may not be purposely trying to ruin your organization, but they're doing it just the same. They're influencing the people around them, for better or worse.

And here's the real point: Since culture is such an enormous factor in any organization's success, is that something we should just leave to chance, and *hope* that the right people are going to influence it? Of course not! It's simply too important to allow it to emerge on its own, following its own path. Instead, as leaders, we should be purposeful and intentional, and even systematic, in our approach to culture. We should *create* the culture we want, rather than live with the culture that emerges by default.

There's an exercise that I sometimes do in my CEO workshops that's pretty revealing. I'll ask the CEOs in attendance to rate the importance of culture, on a scale of 1 to 5, in terms of its impact on the bottom line, with 1 meaning it's not at all important and 5 meaning it has a huge impact. As I go around the room and ask each leader to give me their rating, I usually find that almost everyone will give it a 4 or a 5, and I typically have at least one CEO who will rate it as a 7 or 8 (on a 1 to 5 scale)!

The Fundamentals In Action

Tim Arenberg, the CEO of Columbia Pipe & Supply, a Midwestern distributor of contractor supplies with dozens of branches and hundreds of employees, sees driving the culture as his number-one priority. Says Tim, "Pound for pound, working on culture is the best investment I can make. We've spent millions on other important initiatives, but if we don't get our people all on the same page, working the way we want, nothing else matters. And if we don't have a plan for how to do that, how serious are we about building a lasting differentiation?"

Then I ask them, "How many of you have a written strategic plan that outlines this year's goals, priorities, and strategic initiatives?" They almost all raise their hand. Then I ask, "How many of you have a sales plan that identifies this year's quotas, targets, and how you're going to hit your sales numbers?" Once again, they almost all raise their hands. Then I ask, "How many of you have a documented budget or financial forecast from which you operate?" They all obviously do. Then I ask the kicker: "How many of you have a written, documented, *culture* plan for how you're intentionally driving the culture of your company?"

Usually just one or two people raise their hands—and only about halfway!

"So let me get this straight," I'll tell them. "You just told me that culture was a 5 in terms of its impact on the bottom line, and we're all just winging it, hoping it's going to work out on its own!"

Not having a culture plan would be like trying to run our companies with no budget or forecast and hoping we hit our numbers. Of course, if we had no plan, we'd still be trying to bring in as much money as we could, and we'd still try to be smart about managing our expenses. But the chances that we hit our numbers would certainly be much greater if we were managing to a clearly thought-out and documented plan. The same is true for our culture.

Why don't most leaders create their cultures?

So if culture is so important to organizational success, why don't most leaders take more control over it? In my observation, there are myriad reasons.

It's seen as a "soft" issue. Most leaders are more comfortable talking about issues that seem more concrete—sales, operations, and finance, for example. We have lots of things we can measure and track in these areas, so it's easier to take action and to see progress. How do you measure culture?

It's seen as an HR topic. Many leaders see culture as the domain of the HR department and not the responsibility of the CEO. And yet, as we've seen, culture has an enormous influence on differentiation, productivity, and performance. It's actually a strategic and financial topic more than an HR one, and as such, should be one of the most important areas of focus for the CEO.

It's less controllable. It's relatively easy to create high-quality products and drive out variation in manufacturing processes. Getting *people* to be consistent, though, is much more difficult. People are amazingly variable, and they bring with them a host of idiosyncrasies, issues, and challenges. This can be enormously frustrating.

We never learned how. Most business schools teach leaders about marketing and strategic planning and finance, but not much about culture. And since we're drawn to things we know about, and are therefore comfortable with, we tend to avoid working on culture. We stick to what we know.

It never occurred to us. Believe it or not, most leaders think of culture as something that happens on its own and beyond writing their vision, mission, and values, and trying to set a good example, there isn't much they can really do about it. It's never occurred to them that you can be as intentional and systematic about culture as you can about your sales plan or your financial forecast. They've never seen a methodology for "engineering" culture.

My experience is that we *can* and *should* be intentional about creating and driving the culture we want. And in the coming pages, I'll show you precisely how to do it.

The 8-Step Framework

Before we get started, I want to define a few keys terms that I'll be using throughout this book, beginning with what I call the "Fundamentals System™." The Fundamentals System is a specific methodology and set of tools for creating and "institutionalizing" an organization's culture. When I talk about institutionalizing the culture, I'm referring to getting the culture to be so deeply ingrained in the very fabric of the organization that it can readily be seen in every member of the team. It's part of their DNA. The culture is pervasive in such a way that it's not dependent on just one person. I often use this description to convey what we're trying to achieve and to distinguish it from some people's notion of working on culture as simply having a vision, mission, and set of core values.

I organize the steps that it takes to institutionalize your culture around a framework that I call the "8-Step Framework." It's the same framework that I described in the first chapter of *Fundamentally Different*, though I've changed the order just a bit and I now use the illustration on the next page, rather than simply depicting it as a linear list of steps. In this chapter, I'll introduce you to each of the 8 steps in a rather cursory way, simply because I want you to see the big picture first. In subsequent chapters, I'll take a much deeper dive into each of the steps.

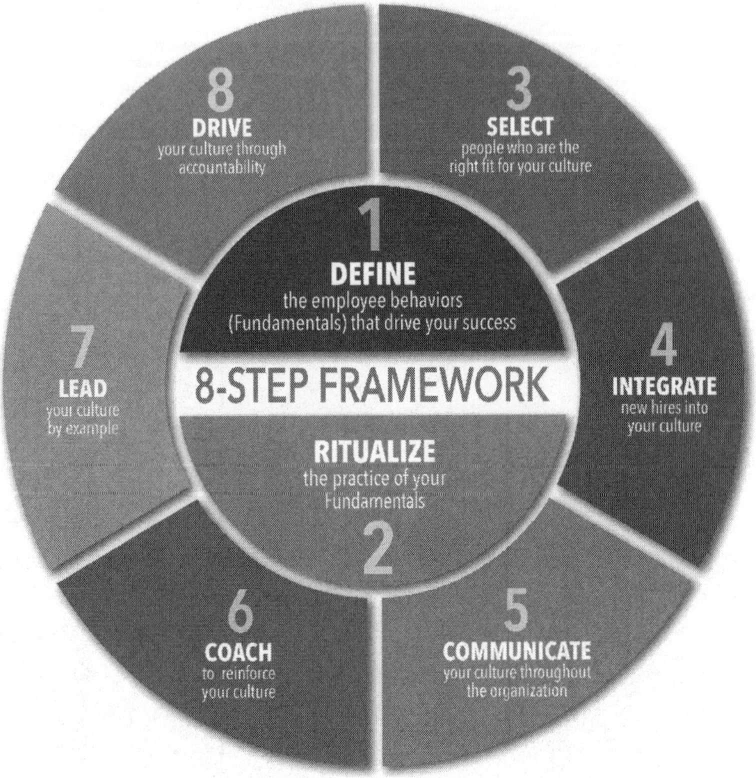

One other note before we begin: While each of the steps in this framework is absolutely important, my experience is that the first two steps, shown in the center of the illustration, have a disproportionate amount of influence over our success. In fact, if we do those two steps well, we'll be at least 80% of the way down the road to success. And if we fail to do those two steps well, we simply won't get very far. Those two steps, as you'll surely see, are really the foundation for the entire concept of the Fundamentals System, and accordingly, I'll be covering them each in a great deal of depth.

Step 1: DEFINE the employee behaviors (Fundamentals) that drive your success

Not surprisingly, we can't begin to create and drive a culture if we can't describe, with tremendous clarity, exactly what we want that culture to be. And yet, as obvious as that may sound, it's remarkable to me how few organizations can truly say exactly what their culture is. They may have a general sense of what it's like—"We're friendly" or "We have a lot of fun" or "We really care about our customers" or "We're collaborative." But this isn't clear enough to be able to teach and institutionalize. Or they may have a stated vision, mission, and set of core values, though I would argue these typically are pretty vague and also don't provide the necessary clarity.

I often say that driving a culture throughout an organization is mostly a teaching function. It's not simply posting the vision and mission. It's about what you and your leadership team are teaching your people day after day after day. And if you don't know what you're teaching, because you've never defined it clearly enough, you're not likely to be able to do it very effectively, and certainly not very consistently.

Building a curriculum

Using that teaching analogy, I often think of defining culture as building a curriculum. Imagine for a moment that, for some reason, you wanted all of your people to be really skillful in math. You go to your managers and supervisors and you tell them, "Starting tomorrow, I want you to teach math to everyone who reports to you." Math is such a broad subject that you might have people teaching a wide variety of topics. One leader might teach algebra while another teaches geometry and another teaches basic skills. And maybe one person is even trying to teach calculus! You'd likely end up with a great deal of disparity in what people learned about math.

Now let's change that story just a bit and assume that you wanted your people to learn not just math, but a subspecialty in math, like algebra. And within algebra, a subtopic, like how to solve quadratic equations. You build an entire curriculum around teaching quadratic equations and you give that curriculum to each of your leaders, asking them to teach that specific curriculum to his/her people. In this scenario, your people would be much more likely to have a consistent knowledge of math, or at least the portion of math you want them to learn.

We can think of culture in much the same way. If driving a culture is mostly a teaching function, then to the extent we can define exactly what we want people to learn, and we can build an entire curriculum around it, we're going to have a greater chance of ensuring that everyone learns the same thing. And ultimately, we're much more likely to see greater organizational consistency.

So the first thing we have to do is to define our culture in absolutely clear terms, and then build a curriculum around it so that everyone is teaching and learning the same thing. In Chapter 4, I'll show you a different and more practical way to accomplish this than you've likely ever considered.

Step 2: RITUALIZE the practice of your Fundamentals

Creating "rituals" is one of the simplest, and yet most powerful, concepts I've ever learned. In fact, it's the key to making things last.

How many new programs or initiatives have we started at work and in our personal lives, determined to make them last, only to see them fall by the wayside as we got busy with "real life?" We've all been there. The danger in rolling out programs that don't last goes beyond simply their diminished effectiveness. Even more importantly, these failures lead to cynicism in our workforce. Our people begin to see every new initiative as the "flavor of the month," and they don't fully engage because they know it will soon be forgotten and/or replaced with a different initiative. Rituals are what enable us to stick with things when we wouldn't normally have the discipline or the motivation to do so on our own.

In Chapter 5, we're going to take an in-depth look at the concept of rituals, how they work, why they're so important, and how we can use them to sustain the teaching and practice of our well-defined culture. As simple as it is, its impact is literally game-changing.

Step 3: SELECT people who are the right fit for your culture

In order for us to build a truly high-performing culture, it's necessary that we become great at choosing people who will be a good fit for that culture. I often say that when people come to your organization to be interviewed or hired, they come to you "fully-baked." In other words, they are who they are. While we can certainly teach them skills, their value system is largely a fait accompli by the time they show up at your door. We're not likely to be able to change much of that.

The implication of this recognition is that we have to start with people who are already a good fit in our culture, because we're not likely to have a lot of success taking people who aren't a good fit and hoping to transform them. While it's possible, the odds are stacked heavily against us in this effort.

In Chapter 6, we'll take a closer look at the selection process. We'll explore what it means to be a "good fit," we'll look at some methods for determining fit, and we'll examine some of the real-world challenges we face in trying to stay disciplined about this important step. We'll also discuss what to do with people you currently have who may not be such a good fit.

Step 4: INTEGRATE new hires into your culture

The fourth element of the 8-Step Framework is what I call "Integration." Integration is what some people call "orientation" or "on-boarding." It's the word that describes the process we use to get our new hires up and running in our organization.

The reason that I use the word "integration" is that it has a different connotation than does "orientation." Orientation suggests that we're telling you about us. We're orienting you to us. Integration, however, is a word of assimilation. It implies that you're becoming one of us.

Regardless of the word you choose to use, how that process is handled has an enormous impact on your organization's culture. In fact, I would argue that a person's first week on the job is literally the most important week in their entire career. It's that impactful.

That first week sets the tone for everything to follow. It's the new person's first impression, and those early impressions tend to be lasting and difficult to change. As impactful as the first week is, it's remarkable how few companies spend appropriate time and resources orchestrating every aspect of a new hire's early experience. Instead, we spend huge amounts of time and money on recruiting, and then give scant attention to how the new person starts.

In Chapter 7, we'll look more closely at the impact of integration, and more importantly, I'll provide you with a host of ideas for how you can better orchestrate a new person's experience to set them up for success and to make a powerful contribution to your culture.

Step 5: COMMUNICATE your culture throughout the organization

As simple as it may sound, the more people see and hear about your culture, the more they think about it, and the more it becomes part of their everyday experience. Visible reminders are particularly important here.

While we've all seen examples of companies that post inspirational quotes or images or clichéd sayings on their walls that seem to bear little resemblance to their organizations' *real* culture, this is not a condemnation of posters. It's a condemnation of the lack of authenticity. If our culture is authentic, the more we see images and reminders of it all around us, the better. You might think of it simply as internal advertising.

In Chapter 8, we'll talk more about why this is so important, and I'll give you lots of examples to spur your own thinking about how you can communicate your culture in a more pervasive way.

Step 6: COACH to reinforce your culture

Throughout this book, I'll often refer to your culture as the actual behavior of your people more so than the statements on your walls. In fact, the best way for me to really know your culture is to observe your people and how they operate every day.

Each day, issues and challenges arise and they make decisions about how to handle them. A customer calls with a problem. A vendor is late with a shipment. Two employees are struggling to get along. How these situations are handled gives a clear indication of your culture.

Your managers and supervisors, of course, are typically providing their teams with coaching and guidance on how to resolve these issues, as well as with feedback on what was done. These coaching sessions are critical opportunities to teach and reinforce the culture. More specifically, every time you use the specific language and vocabulary of the culture in the coaching session, you're pulling the culture off the wall and making it relevant and meaningful. You're showing staff that those words on the wall are real, rather than just being signage.

In Chapter 9, we'll explore the important role that coaching plays in bringing your culture to life, and I'll offer some tips and suggestions on how to increase the effectiveness of that coaching.

Step 7: LEAD your culture by example

Of course, we can talk about our culture as much as we want, and we can display it proudly on our walls, but as leaders, what we actually *do* will always talk much more loudly than what we say. Our people are constantly looking at us, consciously and unconsciously, and they're taking their cues from us about what's really important. How we handle that difficult customer call or that thorny ethical question will tell them much more about our culture than what our posters say.

Whether we like it or not, our people are learning from us every single day. They're learning from what we do, and they're even learning from what we *don't* do.

In Chapter 10, we'll take a closer look at our role as leaders and how it impacts culture. We'll also examine two critical implications that come from understanding the role we play as teachers and how we can leverage this role to better spread our culture.

Step 8: DRIVE your culture through accountability

When I talk about driving accountability in the context of culture, I'm not referring to the general topic of accountability, but rather to being accountable specifically for our culture. In other words, how are we showing ourselves, our people, and the world that we're actually serious about this? For if there's no accountability for it, then it's just a wish.

There are many ways to show just how serious we are, from doing annual surveys on our performance in living to our culture, to including elements of our culture in our performance reviews, to even replacing people who aren't a fit for our culture.

In Chapter 11, I'll give you specific examples and suggestions for creating greater accountability for your culture. These are relatively easy to do, but their impact is huge.

This 8-Step Framework will be our roadmap, and the Fundamentals System our tools, as we start down the path toward more intentionally creating and institutionalizing the culture we want. Now that you understand the big picture, let's begin our deeper exploration by learning how to define our culture with a new level of clarity, and how we can build a curriculum around that culture so that we can teach with greater consistency.

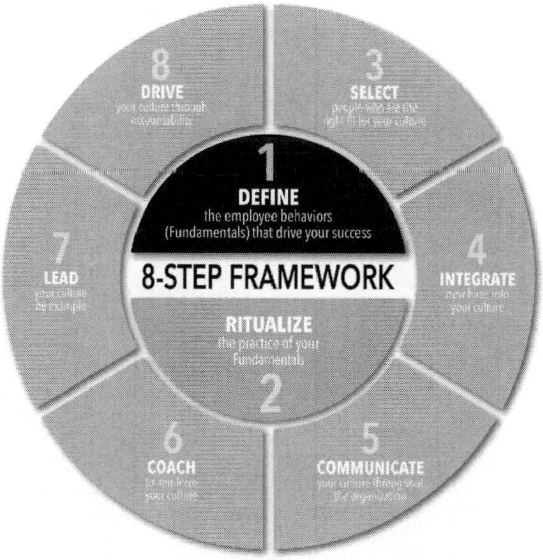

DEFINE the employee behaviors that drive your success

To begin our discussion of how to define our culture with greater clarity than ever before, I need to draw an important language distinction for you. It's a distinction I didn't used to think about, and yet, it's one of the most important premises on which the entire Fundamentals System is built. Specifically, it's the distinction between what I call "values" and what I call "behaviors."

Values vs. behaviors

Interestingly, in *Fundamentally Different*, I used the language of values and behaviors interchangeably, as if they were simply two words for the same idea. In fact, the subtitle of that book is, "Building a culture of success through organizational values." Believe it or not, the first time I began to think about the difference between values and behaviors was when my then 19-year-old son, Ben, challenged me on it. Ben was home from college one summer and agreed to accompany me to one of my workshops. When the program was finished, and we got back into the car, Ben had about ten pages of feedback and questions for me! Perhaps his most important question, though, was this: "I heard you mentioning values and I heard you talk about behaviors. What's the difference?"

My first answer was that they were just two different words that I used for the same concept. But over the next few days I began to think about his question more deeply. And the more I pondered it, the more I began to realize that they were, in fact, very different things, and that their difference was important. Let me explain how they're different and show you why it matters.

Concepts vs. actions

A "value," in the context of culture, is a principle that governs our actions. Examples of values are things like

- Quality
- Integrity
- Respect
- Commitment
- Passion
- Loyalty

These are ideas or notions that we may subscribe to.

A "behavior," in contrast, is an *action.* It's something that I can literally see someone doing. Examples of behaviors are things like

- Practice blameless problem-solving
- Honor commitments
- Be a fanatic about response time
- Get clear on expectations
- Listen generously
- Do what's best for the client

Do you see the difference? Values are ideas or concepts, while behaviors are actions. In an overly simplified way, you might think of a value as a noun (it's a thing) while a behavior is a verb (it's an action).

Note: For those who read Fundamentally Different, you may remember that I called the first ten of our Fundamentals, our "core values." I realize now that they weren't values; they were behaviors. I just wasn't thinking of that distinction at the time.

Wide disparity of definitions

So why does any of this matter? Well, here's the issue: Values, because they tend to be so conceptual or abstract, can mean many different things to many different people. Behaviors though, because they're more action-oriented, tend to be much clearer, and so they're easier to guide, coach, teach, and provide feedback on. Let me share an example to make this point clearer for you.

One of the most common items I see on many companies' list of core values is "Respect." They want to create a culture of respect, where every person is treated respectfully, regardless of their age, position, background, education, or religion. And while this certainly seems like a worthwhile goal, what does "respect" really mean? What it means to you may be quite different than what it means to me.

If you grew up in an inner-city gang, what it means to show someone respect, to earn respect, or to disrespect another person, might be very different than what it means in your family. If you grew up in many areas of the Deep South, you may have been taught to address all adults by saying "Sir" or "Ma'am." In fact, it would be disrespectful to your elders not to address them in this way. But if you grew up in the Northeast, it would be unusual to use those terms, and not using them would imply no disrespect whatsoever.

If you were in a business meeting in Japan, who sits where at the table would be a way of showing respect, and you could inadvertently disrespect someone by sitting in the wrong spot. Recently, I was talking to a friend who's a superintendent of schools in a large public school district. He was lamenting the fact that some teachers feel they're being "disrespected" when they get a salary increase below what they expect. To him, their salary increase is a function of the budget and the available resources. It has nothing to do with respect.

My point, of course, isn't that respect doesn't matter. It's simply that it means so many different things to different people that I don't think the term, used on its own, is particularly helpful. Saying that we value respect or that we want to show everyone respect simply isn't clear enough.

Most values tend to fall into this same trap. What does "loyalty" really mean? How do you define "commitment?" What does "passion" look like to you? Because behaviors are actions, they're usually much clearer to understand and teach.

It may seem like I'm splitting hairs here, or making more of this distinction than is necessary, but as I take you through the entire Fundamentals System, you're going to appreciate why this difference is so important.

Two stories

Let me share with you two stories that helped to crystallize the importance of this distinction in my mind. I often tell these stories in my workshops.

Several years ago, I was giving a talk in the Midwest, and I was staying in a major chain hotel the night before the talk. As is typically the case, very early in the morning on the last day of my stay, an envelope was slipped underneath my door. The envelope contained my receipt for the stay. Like most hotels these days, I knew that I would also get a copy of the receipt sent to me by e-mail within 48-72 hours.

Normally, when I get the e-mailed version, I don't pay a lot of attention to it since I already have the hard copy. However, this particular time it happened to catch my attention because I noticed that the amount that was being charged to my credit card was *different* on the e-mailed receipt from the receipt that had been slipped under my door. And it was more! It wasn't a lot of money, but still, it should have been the same.

Curious to find the discrepancy, I compared the two versions, line-by-line. I quickly realized that the e-mailed version had an extra line. It said, "Room service . . . . $5.35." This made me curious for two reasons. First, I hadn't actually used any room service. And second, have you ever had room service for $5.35?! Something clearly wasn't right.

So I picked up the phone and I called the hotel. The woman who answered was very friendly and she asked how she could help. When I explained the problem to her, she asked me to hold for a moment while she looked over my account. A minute or two later, she got back on and shared with me that the charge in question was for the bottle of Fiji water that was in my room.

While this seemed a lot to pay for a bottle of water, the more important issue was that I didn't actually use the bottle of Fiji water! In fact, traveling as much as I do these days, I'm always on the "concierge" level, where they have free snacks and drinks, and all the water I can consume. When I shared this fact with the woman, she readily acknowledged that it made no sense for me to have drunk the expensive Fiji water, given all the free water available to me. She then went on to explain what *I* could do about it! She told me that the accounting office was closed at the moment, but that she would gladly give me their 800 number and that if I left them a voicemail, they'd likely take it off my bill. Of course, I explained to her an entirely different way we were going to solve this problem!

Here's the point of the story: Do you think the woman I spoke to thought she was giving me good service? I'll bet she did. She explained to me how I could solve my problem. The real issue, however, was that her definition of "good service" was vastly different from my definition.

And here's the larger point: Let's picture this hotel for a moment, and let's assume they have 200 employees. The general manager of the hotel calls a big meeting one day and announces to everyone that she wants to talk about their culture. She shares their vision and their mission and their six core values. Their first value, she explains, is "service." After all, they're in the hospitality business, so what could be more important than delivering fabulous service to their guests? The problem, however, is that if they have 200 employees, they may have 200 different ideas of what great service looks like. So while it's nice to say that one of our core values is service, it's not clear enough to be implemented effectively.

The action form of values

That same year, I was passing through a smaller, regional airport when a sign on the wall caught my attention. The sign listed the airport's vision, mission, and values. I thought this was pretty unusual for an airport, and being in the business, I stopped to read it more closely. They had the typical kind of vision and mission statement that I often see, but when it came to their values, they did something a little different that got me thinking.

I don't remember exactly what their values were, but it was how they were constructed that stood out. Underneath each listed value, there was a series of bullet-pointed statements. It looked something like this:

> We value service. We demonstrate this by doing the following things:
>
> - Statement 1
> - Statement 2
> - Statement 3
>
> We value quality. We demonstrate this by doing the following things:
>
> - Statement 1
> - Statement 2
> - Statement 3

And so on. Each of their values included clear statements that described the observable behaviors that helped give the values life and meaning. In fact, you might think of behaviors as "values in action." They're the action form of the value. They're what you do to live to or demonstrate the value. I thought that was a pretty smart approach, and ultimately, a much more useful one than simply creating the standard list of one-word core values.

Two methods for defining your culture

Having worked with hundreds of companies across the country in so many different industries, helping them to more clearly define what they want their culture to be, I've discovered that there are many different approaches we could take to this process. But there are two methods in particular that I've found to be effective.

The first method follows the airport's approach. We could define the core values that are important to us, and then for each value, we could write the corresponding behaviors that help us to live to that value or to demonstrate it in action. This approach is very straightforward and logical, and brings valuable clarity to how you define your culture.

There's another approach, however, that I used in my first company, without knowing about any of this, and it's actually what all our clients use. Now this is one of those places I warned you about where I'm going to suggest something that flies in the face of conventional wisdom and may sound almost sacrilegious, so try to keep an open mind and allow me to explain the logic. And remember that it's worked hundreds of times with companies who at first wanted to reject it.

In the second method, we skip the discussion of our values and we simply go directly to our behaviors. In other words, we describe the behaviors that we want to define our culture, without any need to tie them back to particular values.

Now here's where it gets really interesting. I used to say to people that either of those approaches is fine. If it works better for you, and you feel more comfortable organizing your behaviors around a set of values, then go right ahead. And if you'd prefer to skip the extra step, and more directly identify the behaviors without reference to the values, well that's fine too. Since we're still articulating behaviors either way, and that's the most important part, it doesn't really matter how you get there. Right? Wrong.

While I used to suggest that either approach was fine, I no longer say that because I discovered something very interesting. It turns out that those two approaches will actually yield two different lists of behaviors! It was fascinating when I began to realize this and thought more deeply about why this happens.

Introducing a filter or constraint

When we use the airport method, notice that we're actually introducing a limiter or a constraint into our thinking. In other words, we're *limiting* ourselves to thinking only of the behaviors that tie directly to the values in question. An example may help you to see this more clearly.

In the airport method, we start by asking ourselves, "What are our values? What are the principles that we hold dear?" To make the illustration simple, let's assume that we identified four core values: Integrity, Quality, Excellence, and Service.

Then we ask ourselves, "What do we mean by 'integrity?' What are the specific behaviors that help us to demonstrate our vision of integrity?" Let's assume that we're able to articulate four behaviors that make our definition of integrity much clearer. We then follow the same path for quality, excellence, and service. We now have four important values, and we've defined each in terms of the specific behaviors that help us to live to those values. Life is good.

But here's the problem: It turns out that there are behaviors that are really important to our success that *fall outside* the scope of the four values we identified. And we're never even going to think about those behaviors or talk about them because we limited ourselves to considering only items that were tied directly to the four values in question. I often use the drawing on the following page to illustrate this phenomenon in a visual way.

Behaviors A, B, C, and D may be critically important to success, but because they fall outside of the boxes for Integrity, Quality, Excellence, and Service, we're not likely to consider them!

To be clear, I'm not suggesting that these two approaches are diametrically opposed. In fact, they may overlap by 85%. But there may be 15% of behaviors that fall outside the scope of those previously identified values, and yet are significant drivers of success, and they're never going to be on the table for discussion. Some examples may help you to see this more clearly.

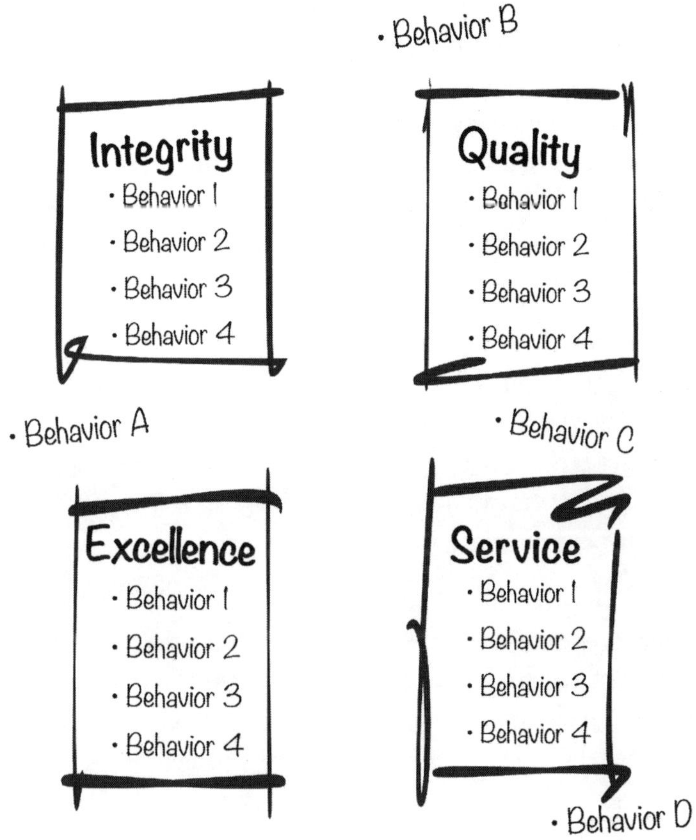

Two examples

One of the behaviors that was core to us at RSI was a behavior (we call them "Fundamentals") that I called "Set and ask for expectations." These days, I usually just call it "Get clear on expectations." I've always taught that we judge situations not by what happened, but rather by how it compared to what we *expected* to happen. In fact, almost every misunderstanding comes from two people having different expectations about what was to occur. There are lots of reasons for this, and I wrote an entire chapter on it in *Fundamentally Different*, but suffice it to say that if we take the extra time to be more rigorous in our language and make sure that in every conversation we're crystal clear about the expectations, our effectiveness as individuals and as an organization improves dramatically. This is such a foundational principle that I virtually insist that it be included in the Fundamentals for every one of our clients.

So which value would that behavior fit under? To be honest, I have no idea, and I really don't care! I just know I want my people to do it. To take it a step further, if I had written my core values first, and only considered those behaviors that fell under the values, would I ever have thought about "Set and ask for expectations"? Possibly, but probably not. And yet it was really important to our success.

Here's another Fundamental that I insist be included for every one of our clients: "Practice blameless problem solving." In my observation, one of the biggest causes of organizational dysfunction is blame. So many people are more focused on avoiding blame, defending themselves, protecting themselves, covering up mistakes, and blaming others than they are fixing problems and learning. When we change that dynamic and we address problems quickly, learn from them, and improve our processes as a result of what we learned—without worrying about blame—the difference is remarkable. It's an incredibly powerful behavior. Once again, which value does that fit under and would it ever come up if we started with our values and only defined behaviors in relation to those values?

It turns out that there are a number of behaviors like these two that might be critical to our success that would never come up for discussion if we limited ourselves to only considering those behaviors that tied directly to our values.

Going in reverse?

Sometimes people ask me about going in reverse. In other words, couldn't we come up with our list of behaviors without restriction, and then see what values are implied or are inherent in those behaviors? My response is that we might be able to do that, but I'm not sure I see a good reason to try. Our ultimate goal is to define behaviors, as that's what will most effectively provide the necessary clarity to operationalize our culture. If we already have the behaviors, what's the point in going backwards? What purpose does that serve?

From a purely practical standpoint, it's also very frustrating because you end up trying to force behaviors into categories where they don't really fit, or you have some behaviors that might fit into several different categories. Ultimately, it's just not necessary.

Others argue that the values, being broader, give you an "umbrella" under which to capture behaviors you might not have called out specifically. In other words, they suggest that the values give people broad guidance so that as long as they're operating in a way that's consistent with the value, they know their actions are acceptable. While this makes some sense, when I explain how we're going to go about defining the behaviors, you'll see that, when pitched at the right level, the behaviors will accomplish this goal quite nicely. Trust me on this point for now, and I'm confident you'll see what I mean as we progress.

Another argument I sometimes hear for grouping behaviors under values is that the values, being fewer in number, will be easier to remember. While I don't disagree with this assertion, the goal isn't simply to memorize them, but rather to *live* them daily. And as you'll see shortly, the way we teach and practice the behaviors through the Fundamentals System makes memorization unnecessary and unimportant.

For readers who feel particularly uncomfortable about "letting go" of values, let me be clear. I'm not suggesting that values don't matter or that they have no impact. It's actually quite the opposite. We all have values in our hearts and minds, and these values absolutely influence how we behave. They're influencing us, whether we've articulated them or not. I'm simply saying that while the values certainly exist, from an operational standpoint, listing or defining them isn't nearly as useful as defining the *behaviors* that we want to see practiced in our organizations. The behaviors are much easier to teach, coach, and guide. They're how we actually operationalize the culture.

I'm going to show you how to think of the behaviors that are important to you and how to write them clearly, but first, I want to identify three mistakes that companies frequently make when doing this work. By calling these mistakes out in advance, I'm hopeful that you can avoid falling into these traps.

Mistake 1: Too much collaboration

The first mistake I see too many organizations make in defining their culture is being too collaborative. Now this may sound odd to you, as many consultants advocate a process where you get the input of all the various "stakeholders" to determine the culture, from employees to customers, and sometimes even key business partners. They argue that this helps to ensure the culture you're creating is responsive to all the key constituencies, and helps to increase employee engagement.

I take a very different view. Beyond the obvious concern that including too many people can water down the result or cause us to solve for the lowest common denominator, there's a more foundational issue. At its core, defining the culture is a *leadership* function. In fact, it's one of the most important functions and responsibilities of a leader. Great leaders call out a compelling vision and then enlist people and marshal the resources to pursue and achieve that vision. They don't ask the organization where it would like to go. They create the vision and then make it happen.

I often call this a "design function." We're designing the extraordinary company that we want to create. We're not designing it around the wishes or desires of all the people who we coincidentally employ today. Rather, we're designing it around our vision of what we want to build.

Having said that, I'm actually a big advocate for the inclusion of the senior leadership team in this process. But let me be crystal clear about their role. I'm a big advocate for including them *for their contribution to the leader's thinking.* Notice the words in italics. They're contributing to the leader's thinking. They're on the team because they're smart and they have good ideas and they have a lot to add to the leader's thinking. This isn't to make them feel good. They're being included because their contribution is valuable. But at the end of the day, it's the leader's responsibility to decide which behaviors get included and which don't. It's not a majority vote, and it's not a consensus. It's the leader who decides the vision.

For those who may be concerned that this "top down" approach won't ever work because employees haven't been engaged in the process, my experience is that employees get incredibly engaged in how the Fundamentals get rolled out. The engagement of the workforce is absolutely important. The mistake is in thinking that the only way to achieve that engagement is to include everyone in the design phase. As you'll see, the rollout process that I describe in Chapter 12 creates amazing engagement throughout the entire organization.

I should offer one other "qualifier" to my comments about over-collaboration here: Most of my experience is with privately-held, entrepreneurial organizations, rather than public companies or others who may have Boards. In these cases, depending on your Board relationship, you may want to include Board members as contributors to the initial brainstorming, or even in the rollout process. Here again, while their support and advocacy is important, it's the leader's vision that should ultimately drive the culture.

Mistake 2: Writing clichés

Too often I see organizations come up with a list of values or behaviors that include clichés that may sound good, but don't actually mean much. My best example of this is when we say that we're committed to "exceeding our customers' expectations." I see this statement framed in board rooms, listed on websites, and even painted on company trucks; and while it may sound powerful, are we really serious about it? I doubt it.

If we were, we'd surely be documenting every customer's expectations, for how could we be sure we're exceeding them if we don't even know what they are? And we'd definitely be measuring the degree to which we exceeded them, since that's one of our most important goals. And of course, if we kept exceeding their expectations, they would keep raising them and it would eventually become virtually impossible to continue exceeding them!

The goal in defining behaviors isn't to capture fancy buzzwords or phrases, rather it's to capture what truly matters to you. The key is to look *inside* yourself to identify the things that are meaningful to you. Here are some good questions to ask yourself to get you started:

- What are the things that, if done more consistently, would make your company amazing?
- What are the things that you often "rant" about? If you're not sure, ask those around you. (After all, you wouldn't rant about them if they weren't important to you.)
- What are the things that drive you crazy when you see them happening? If they drive you crazy, you have some energy and passion around them. What's the opposite of those behaviors? In other words, what would you like people to be doing instead of doing that which drives you crazy?
- Typically, in every department, we have at least one or more people who we wish we could clone. Think of the specific people you wish you could clone. What do they do that makes you want to clone them? Those are likely to be important behaviors. (Often it helps to visualize real people rather than trying to think of behaviors in the abstract.)

The reason this is so important is that it's very difficult to be a true and authentic leader of behaviors you really don't believe in, but have included because you heard them somewhere. And conversely, it's easy to be an authentic leader of the behaviors you're always talking about. The goal is to capture what's authentically you and write it down.

Mistake 3: Writing this as a marketing piece

One of the most common mistakes I see is trying to write this as a marketing piece. In other words, we try to codify our culture primarily for a customer audience. "You should buy from us because these are our five core values." I don't know about you, but I've never bought from a company because I read their core values. While I suppose it might possibly cause me to feel an affinity for them, I buy because they offer the right combination of price, product, and/or service.

This is not a marketing piece. This is the curriculum we're writing for what we want to teach our people. This is the owner's manual or the instruction manual for what it looks like to be a fabulous employee in our company. In other words, we're writing to our own employees, not to our customers.

To be clear, there's nothing at all wrong with sharing it with customers. At High Performing Culture, we share our Fundamentals with customers all the time, as do virtually all our clients. It's how we talk about our culture, and it does become a point of differentiation. However, I would have written them differently if I was writing to our customers versus writing to my own employees.

If there are certain phrases or lingo that are common in your organization, this would be a good place to use them. At RSI, we had a Fundamental that we called "Practice A+ness as a way of life." It was a phrase that we used all the time and it meant something very clear and specific to our people. It didn't matter to me whether our customers understood it. It was written for our own people. The more you use your own language, the more it resonates with your people, rather than it sounding like "consultant speak." In short, keep it real.

Brand vs. culture

One of the reasons I think organizations, and the consultants who work with them, make mistake #3 so frequently is that they confuse a "branding exercise" with a "culture exercise." In a branding exercise, we're trying to articulate for the marketplace what makes us different from our competitors. In a culture exercise, we're trying to articulate the rules of engagement for how to be a fantastic contributor in our organization. While there could be some overlap, they have two very different goals. Let me share an example.

I was working with a client, facilitating the process of developing their Fundamentals, and the topic of acting with integrity arose. It's a very important behavior that almost always comes up, and I strongly encourage it to be included for all our clients. The CEO was a little confused because they had recently gone through a branding project with a marketing consultant and the consultant suggested that integrity shouldn't be listed as a brand differentiator because it was virtually assumed. In other words, it was simply a given, or a "price of admission" just to have a seat at the table.

From a branding perspective, I totally agree with the consultant. Integrity *is* just assumed and isn't going to separate you from your competitors (at least the worthy ones). However, from a culture perspective, acting with integrity is an absolutely essential behavior that we should call out and teach and reinforce for the rest of our careers. As soon as we stop talking and teaching about acting with integrity, we run the risk of unethical behavior beginning to creep into our organizations.

Remember that branding is mostly targeted to our customers, while culture is mostly for our employees. As we articulate the behaviors we want to define our culture, we're writing to our own employees.

Developing your Fundamentals

With those mistakes out of the way, we're ready to learn how to define, with tremendous clarity, those behaviors you want to drive your culture. Before we dive in though, let me make one comment about nomenclature. I think it's helpful to have a name for our behaviors, as it gives them extra weight and importance. When I first developed this process at RSI, I chose the name "Fundamentals" because I thought these behaviors were fundamental to our success. Most of the companies we've worked with have followed suit and use that same name, and it's why I call the suite of methods, tools, training, and resources for institutionalizing your culture, the "Fundamentals System." We do have a few clients who use other names (e.g., Basics, Tenets, Principles), but most use Fundamentals. For simplicity, throughout the rest of this book I'm going to use the word "Fundamentals" as an alternative for the word "behaviors."

Who should be included?

As I noted earlier, while the responsibility for authoring your culture lies with the CEO, I strongly recommend the inclusion of the senior leadership team for their "contribution to your thinking." Depending on the size of your organization, this is typically a group of roughly 5–8 people. If your leadership group is smaller, that's fine. You just want to make sure there are enough people to get some dialogue and discussion going, and to get a variety of ideas on the table. If your group is larger, or if there are certain political dynamics that make it necessary or advisable to include more people, that's OK as well. The faci... tion process can get a little clumsy when there are too many people, but I'd sooner have a few more people than exclude someone whose contributions and/or buy-in may prove valuable.

I'm sometimes asked about including non-management folks who may be influential workers among their peers, or who may be part of a "culture committee" consisting primarily of non-management employees. Here again, I'd follow the same guidelines as above. If you think their contribution will be significant and/or their participation will facilitate greater adoption among your workforce, then I'd err on the side of including them.

Establishing clear ground rules

Let me offer a warning here about a common mistake leaders make with regard to collaboration. You gather a group of team members and ask them to participate in a project. They contribute their ideas or feedback and then you choose to follow a different course or to accept some of their ideas and not others. The team members leave grumbling about why you even bothered to ask for their input since you weren't going to use it anyway. Does that sound familiar?

The mistake is in not setting clear expectations (a common Fundamental, by the way) around the role you're asking people to play in the process. Decisions can be made in a variety of ways. Sometimes it's best to vote and have the majority decide. Sometimes it's best to build a consensus. And sometimes you simply want input but you're going to make the final decision. Any of these approaches can be perfectly appropriate for different situations. The problem comes when participants thought they were playing by one set of rules and you had in mind a different set. In this specific case, if you're the leader, it's important to let everyone know that their role is to contribute to your thinking and that you'll be making the final decision.

Brainstorming behaviors

Once you have your team together, I'd suggest setting aside 3–4 hours for the brainstorming process. It can be helpful to have a facilitator guide the process so that you can participate fully without having to spend time or energy thinking about the group dynamics.

While you may likely have some legacy materials you previously created around your vision, mission, or core values, for the purpose of this exercise, I think it best to set those aside and begin with a clean slate. Allow yourself the ability to think freely, without being influenced by that previous work. When your list is complete, you can always look back at any previous materials as a reference point to ensure that you've covered everything that's important to you.

I like to begin the brainstorming process by asking some of the questions I listed earlier in this chapter. I'll repeat them here for your ease of use:

- What are the things that, if done more consistently, would make your company amazing?
- What are the things that you often "rant" about? If you're not sure, ask those around you. (After all, you wouldn't rant about them if they weren't important to you.)
- What are the things that drive you crazy when you see them happening? If they drive you crazy, you have

some energy and passion around them. What's the opposite of those behaviors? In other words, what would you like people be doing instead of doing that which drives you crazy?

- Typically, in every department, we have at least one or more people who we wish we could clone. Think of the specific people you wish you could clone. What do they do that makes you want to clone them? Those are likely to be important behaviors. (Often it helps to visualize real people rather than trying to think of behaviors in the abstract.)

With these questions on the table, you can now allow your group to contribute their ideas. As you hear ideas, have someone record them on a whiteboard or on a flip chart. It's important at this stage not to worry about wordsmithing; just get the idea recorded. Though we're not trying to wordsmith, it *is* still important to make sure we're clear about what the speaker means. Asking some clarifying questions for that purpose is perfectly appropriate, and can be quite helpful.

One of the clarifying questions I'm often posing is "What do you want people to actually *do*?" Or said another way, "What does this look like *in action*?" For example, sometimes I'll hear a leader say, "There needs to be more accountability around here." While that may sound good, I'm not really sure what that means in terms of the specific behavior they're asking for. I might ask, "What would you see someone doing that you would say they're demonstrating accountability?" This may lead to a clearer behavior such as, "I want people to take ownership for issues rather than waiting for someone else to solve the problem." I would then write down "Take ownership."

Keep writing down behaviors for as long as people have ideas. I often describe this process as similar to cooking microwave popcorn. When you begin, there will be lots of ideas popping from everyone. Eventually, the ideas begin to slow until there's just one popping here and another one there. Don't worry about how many behaviors you wrote down; just capture what's important. I'll show you in the next chapter why the total number isn't a big deal.

As you go through the process of brainstorming your behaviors, here are some things to keep in mind:

Pitched at the right level

Behaviors, of course, exist on a variety of levels, and it's important that we're working at the right level in this brainstorming exercise. In an overly simplified way, I think of behaviors as being one of three types:

1. **SOPs** – Standard Operating Procedures, or SOPs, are tactical actions that you want people to take. For example, "Make seven sales calls each week" or "Submit your expense reports with 30 days." While these are essential rules to follow for a successful company, they're not a definition of our culture.
2. **Management Principles** – Management principles are guidelines that we want to follow from a corporate perspective, but they usually apply only to leaders or managers. For example, "We want to empower our people" or "We want to hire the best talent available." Here again, these are important principles, but our Fundamentals should be actions that apply to all our employees.
3. **Principle-based Behaviors** – "Principle-based behaviors" are behaviors that apply to all people, but operate

at the level of a principle. For example, "Honor commitments" is a principle, but it's an action. "Practice blameless problem-solving" is a principle, but it's an action. This is the level of behavior that we're looking for.

One set of Fundamentals

We should be able to create one set of Fundamentals that applies to all departments throughout the organization. In other words, we don't want to have one set for the sales department and another for the service department, nor do we want to have some Fundamentals that are only relevant for one unit. The best way to overcome this tendency is to "elevate" the behavior to the larger principle.

For example, sometimes I'll hear, "I hate when we have mistakes on our proposals. I want the sales people to double-check their quotes before they send them." While double-checking quotes is important, the larger principle here might be called "Pay attention to the details" or "Do it right the first time." Paying attention to the details would be as applicable for the receptionist as it is for the salesperson or someone in the plant, or the warehouse, or a truck driver.

While we want to state the Fundamental in a way that's broad enough to apply to everyone, we want to teach it to people in a way that's context specific. What it means to "Be a fanatic about response time" is different if you're a salesperson or a receptionist or a bookkeeper, but the overriding principle is just as applicable. We just want to teach it in a way that's relevant and meaningful to the person in question.

Strengths and areas for improvement

Earlier in this chapter, I described creating the culture you want as a "design function." What I mean by this is that we're trying to envision the extraordinary organization we want to create, and then we're taking the steps to bring that vision to fruition.

If we already have a pretty good company (and most readers of this book probably do), our vision for the future probably borrows heavily from who we are today. There are likely many behaviors that have been foundations for our success, and we don't ever want to stop teaching them. We want to make sure that we capture those so that we can codify them and institutionalize them. In addition, there are likely a fair number of things we need to do better or differently in the future to achieve our vision. We want to capture those as well. So the definition of the culture we want to create is usually a combination of both the behaviors that have led to our success so far as well as the behaviors we need to improve upon.

Categories of behaviors

While it's not necessary to group your Fundamentals into any kind of categories, thinking of behaviors in categories helps some people to brainstorm better. If you find that helpful, here are four categories you might consider to spur your thinking:

1. *How we work with customers* – These are Fundamentals that describe customer-focused behaviors. For example, "Deliver legendary service" or "Be a fanatic about response time."

2. *How we work with each other* – These are Fundamentals that describe ways of working together more successfully. For example, "Practice blameless problem solving" or "Share information."
3. *How we do our own work* – These are Fundamentals that address the way we approach our work. For example, "Demonstrate a passion for excellence" or "Be relentless about improvement."
4. *Our attitude* – These are Fundamentals that describe the attitude that we display. For example, "Embrace change" or "Assume positive intent."

How unique should our Fundamentals be?

Having taken hundreds of organizations through this process, it's not surprising that I've seen a lot of commonality among Fundamentals. I say that it's not surprising because companies are companies and people are people. In other words, what it takes to get a group of people to come together and perform in extraordinary ways isn't very different whether it's an engineering firm or an IT company or a construction company or a non-profit social service agency. As a result, there is a core group of Fundamentals that should be in virtually every company, and then many others that also appear frequently across a wide variety of organizations. In fact, if you looked at the Fundamentals for many of our clients, you probably wouldn't be able to guess what industry they're in.

To be sure, there are a few behaviors that might be unique to an organization. For example, those companies involved in manufacturing or construction will frequently have a Fundamental about safety, where a service business typically would not. And one CEO may have a strong conviction about a behavior that another CEO feels less passionate about. But most Fundamentals aren't very different from one organization to another.

Having said that, I still find that the process of brainstorming the Fundamentals is an essential one. When you've thought of the ideas yourself, even if those ideas aren't all that unique, you'll feel more ownership and commitment to them than if you simply looked at a list of potential Fundamentals and picked the ones you liked the most, like choosing from a menu at a Chinese restaurant.

And remember our discussion about the difference between a branding exercise and a culture exercise. In a branding exercise, we're trying to describe for the marketplace what makes us unique. A culture exercise isn't so much about uniqueness as it is about organizational effectiveness. What it takes to be incredibly effective isn't all that unique. It's just that most organizations don't teach and practice the essential behaviors with enough consistency. In fact, I often say that the best people and organizations don't do anything that's so unusual; instead, they do what I call "ordinary things with *extraordinary* consistency."

Write explanatory descriptions

Once your brainstorming is complete, it's important to write a brief description for each Fundamental. The description should be 2–4 sentences that serve to explain a little more fully what you mean by that behavior. For example,

> **HONOR COMMITMENTS.** Do what you say you're going to do, when you say you're going to do it. If a commitment can't be fulfilled, notify others early and agree upon a new deliverable to be honored.

Notice how the description provides more clarity than does the simple two-word title. It explains what we mean by honoring our commitments. The description need not answer every question that might arise about the Fundamental. This isn't the place for it, nor would it even be possible. Throughout this book, we'll be discussing many other tools and opportunities for more robust teaching. This is simply a brief explanation that helps the reader to understand the essence of the Fundamental.

The bulk of the description should explain the actions you want to see people take, rather than being what I call "philosophical" statements. A philosophical statement is a statement of your belief or philosophy about the principle. For example, "Honoring commitments is critical to delivering great service." This may be a true statement, but it doesn't describe the action.

This is not to suggest that all philosophical statements should be avoided. Some are OK as they may add depth or nuance to the description, but the bulk of the description should be action oriented. Here's an example of a description that's mostly action, but includes an additional statement.

> **EMBRACE CHANGE.** What got us here is not the same as what will get us to the next level. Be inspired by the opportunities that change brings, rather than stubbornly holding on to old ways of doing things. Be flexible and open to new approaches.

Notice how the first statement isn't an action, but it helps to provide context for the action statements that follow. Again, make sure that the majority of the description explains the actions that give meaning to the title.

Make all titles actions

It's also important to make sure that every title is itself an action. While this may sound overly picky, it's a much more powerful statement when described in terms of action. The title "**OWNERSHIP**" is simply an idea. I may be in favor of it, or I may think it's a good thing, but it doesn't call me to do anything. The title "**TAKE OWNERSHIP**" is an action. It's an instruction. It tells me what to do.

When I created my original list of Fundamentals, I wasn't thinking about this difference, and so a few of my titles were written as declarative statements rather than actions. For example, Fundamental #25 at RSI was called "**BEING ORGANIZED MAKES A DIFFERENCE**." Notice that there's no action being called for (though, of course, I did include actions in the full description). Today, I call that same Fundamental, "**BE OBSESSIVE ABOUT ORGANIZATION**." It has much more power to it when written in this way.

Avoid "We statements"

The first time I helped a company (outside of my own) to write a set of Fundamentals, I made what I later realized was another mistake. I wrote each title as what I call a "We statement." For example, "**WE HONOR OUR COMMITMENTS**" or "**WE PRACTICE BLAMELESS PROBLEM-SOLVING**." I thought it would sound more inclusive if I wrote it that way.

While it might have that impact, it actually serves to weaken the statement. When it's written as a statement of what we all do, it doesn't speak to me as individual and give me any personal direction or investment. Have you ever heard the phrase, "Shared accountability is no accountability"? If no one specific person has accountability, we all look to someone else for it. In the same way, if we all honor our commitments, it doesn't speak to me about my personal responsibility.

The same warning applies to our descriptions. Make sure the sentences in your descriptions explain what you want people to do, rather than making statements about what "we" do.

Picture a real person

As you think about how to write a good description, it's often helpful to picture real people in your organization. If you're trying to articulate the actions that describe "**TAKE OWNERSHIP**," picture some of your best people. Do you have anyone who you think is the world's greatest icon for taking ownership? If so, what does that person do that makes you say that? That becomes most of your description. If you don't currently have anyone who's a good example of this Fundamental, imagine you hired someone who was. What would they be doing that would cause you to say, "Wow! This person really gets this Fundamental"? The more accurately you can describe what you want to see people do, the easier it will be for people to understand it, and the easier it will be to teach and coach it.

Keep it positive

In most cases, it's better to describe what you *want* people to do, rather than what you don't want them to do. Instead of

"Don't be late," it's more helpful to say, "Be on time." Give people a picture to live up to rather than a list of things to avoid. This is true both for the title of the Fundamental as well as the description.

While this is a good rule of thumb in most cases, there are some rare times when the negative form may be stronger, clearer, or more compelling. I've worked with a few companies in the food industry and we've included a Fundamental that we call, "**NEVER COMPROMISE ON FOOD SAFETY**." This is a clearer and more powerful statement than if we tried to turn it into a positive.

Within the body of a description, I also sometimes use a negative statement if it helps to add clarity, but the bulk of the description should help the reader to know what you *want* them to do more than all the things you *don't* want them to do.

One behavior at a time

Be careful not to combine too many ideas or behaviors into one Fundamental. The test I use to determine whether behaviors should be listed separately or combined is to think about whether the teaching around the component parts is robust enough that I'd hate to lose the chance to focus on each part because I blended it with other ideas.

For example, communication comes up as a major issue for almost every company. A Fundamental like "**COMMUNICATE EFFECTIVELY**" is too broad because there are so many things that need to be taught inside of that. Virtually all of our clients have at least three different Fundamentals related to effective communication. We call them:

- **LISTEN GENEROUSLY**
- **SPEAK STRAIGHT**
- **GET CLEAR ON EXPECTATIONS**

Each of these behaviors has so much teaching content that we would risk the ability to focus deeply on them if they were combined into a broad discussion of communication.

Sometimes the ideas are sufficiently similar enough that we don't lose much by combining them. For example, in my original set of Fundamentals at RSI, I had both "**HONOR COMMITMENTS**" and "**BE PUNCTUAL**." Today, I would be more inclined to combine those as I view being on time as an example of honoring a commitment. I don't think we lose much by focusing on honoring our commitments and teaching the importance of being on time within that context.

How many behaviors should we have?

The question of how many Fundamentals is the "right" number is probably the question I'm asked most frequently, and it's also the one that surprises people the most. Let me start by saying that, of course, there is no "right" number. You should have whatever number of Fundamentals is necessary to cover the behaviors you think are most important to teach and practice in your organization. And to a certain degree, the number really doesn't matter much.

Having said that, I can share with you that having led hundreds of organizations through this process, the fewest I've ever seen is 20, and the most I've ever seen is 40. The average number of Fundamentals is between 25 and 30. My original list from RSI had 30, as does my list for High Performing Culture. I can also tell you that virtually every one of those companies thought, in advance, that any more than five or ten would be too difficult and would never work. None of those companies is saying that today.

Though this sounds counterintuitive, I promise that it will make perfect sense to you when you understand what we're going to do with these Fundamentals. Stay tuned, as I'll cover that in Chapter 5.

While the number isn't a major concern, there *is* still some outer limit where it begins to become unwieldy and perhaps overwhelming. As you look through the results of your brainstorming, you'll see that not every one of the ideas that was suggested has the same level of importance to you. That's the nature of brainstorming. You should feel free to eliminate those that you deem to be not as critical.

As a general rule, I try not to go over 30. At the same time, the most relevant issue is to capture what you think is important to success. If you get your list down to 31 Fundamentals and there's nothing you want to give up, then I'd encourage you stick to 31 rather than letting go of something important just to get to an arbitrary number like 30.

An intention of permanence

Another question I'm often asked is whether we should expect our Fundamentals to change over time or even whether we should schedule periodic reviews of them to explore appropriate additions or changes. My answer here may surprise you as well.

The best way to describe the recommended approach is to say that we should work on our Fundamentals with what I call an "intention of permanence." In other words, we should put the amount of time and effort into getting it right that would be appropriate if we were expecting it to last forever. We're not simply "getting something out there," figuring we'll adjust as we go. Nor are we planning on reviewing them every year or every five years.

If these behaviors are truly foundational to our success, they *should be* enduring. In fact, in a changing, chaotic, tumultuous world, it gives people a sense of security to know that they can rely on the Fundamentals as a stable foundation for their work life.

For those who argue that we need to be flexible and responsive to our changing environment, I would suggest that the changing conditions should cause us to regularly evaluate our products and services, our strategy, our priorities, and our key initiatives to ensure that we stay relevant. But our culture remains the same. After all, what would change in our marketplace that would have us no longer wanting to honor our commitments or to practice blameless problem solving or to get clear on expectations? These (and other Fundamentals) are foundational elements of success that actually help us to stay responsive to a changing world.

With regard to adding Fundamentals, rather than changing them, my experience is that if we created a good set of Fundamentals from the beginning, anything new that we might want to teach could likely fit somewhere within our existing set.

At the same time, I do use the word "intention" of permanence for a reason. It is literally an intention, a plan, a desire. If something comes up that's so important that you must change your Fundamentals, by all means you should do so. They're there to serve you, not the other way around. It's just that we should go there carefully.

A good analogy is that of the U.S. Constitution. We've relied heavily on the Constitution for more than 200 years with relatively few changes. Further, we don't review it regularly to see what changes we might want to make. At the same time, the Constitution does provide a mechanism through which amendments can be adopted, but it's purposely an arduous and lengthy process. This helps to ensure that we make changes only with great care and thought.

At RSI, we practiced our original Fundamentals for many years without changing a single word. While I certainly learned things and could have made some improvements, I felt that the value of the permanence outweighed the value of the small tweaks I could have made.

What do we do with our previous core values?

In my experience, most organizations have, at some point in their history, created some statements about their culture—perhaps a vision or mission or a set of core values. What to do with those legacy statements can be a perplexing question as you embrace the Fundamentals approach. Let me offer you an easy way to resolve this dilemma that's worked beautifully for so many others.

Broadly speaking, organizations who've done previous work on culture typically fall into two large buckets. The first are those who came up with a vision, mission, and values, perhaps even working with a consultant, put them on their website, and then rarely, if ever, talk about them. Most employees probably couldn't recite any of it, and it plays no meaningful role in how the company functions. Sadly, this represents the majority of organizations. In these cases, I simply suggest that you forget about the previous work and start fresh by implementing the Fundamentals System.

The other bucket includes those organizations whose leaders, perhaps the ones more likely to be reading this book, have been quite serious about their culture. They may have a set of core values that they worked hard on, that are meaningful for them, and that they talk about frequently. In these cases, we don't want to simply go to our employees and tell them "Never mind! Forget everything we've been saying about our culture. We have a new plan." So how can we adopt the more practical approach of the Fundamentals System without having to give up everything we've done before?

> **The Fundamentals In Action**
>
> Field Fastener, headquartered outside of Chicago, is a distributor of industrial fasteners, with approximately 140 team members working in Chicago, Texas, and two facilities in Mexico. Notes the CEO, Jim Derry, "We had put a significant emphasis on our core values but were trying to figure out how to make them clearer. The Fundamentals System gave us the method to describe the behaviors that are important to our culture and helped us to be more consistent across all our locations. We've even converted them to Spanish and have rolled this out in Mexico. While we didn't let go of our core values, we describe our 'Fieldamentals' as the way in which we *live to* our core values."

Here's my recommendation: As I noted earlier in this chapter, when we develop our Fundamentals, we do so with a clean slate, not limited or influenced by any previous work we may have done. We then check our previous statements to be sure that everything that's important to us has been addressed in the Fundamentals. When we roll out our Fundamentals to the organization, we describe them as the daily practices that bring our values to life. It might sound something like this:

> "As you know, our culture is one of the most important ingredients in our success. And the five core values that we've always talked about are what define that culture. But what do those values mean in action? These 30 Fundamentals describe the day-to-day behaviors that help give those values life."

We're describing the Fundamentals as the way in which we live to our values. To be clear, we're not trying to "map" the Fundamentals to our values. In other words, we're not saying that Fundamentals 1-6 equal Value 1 and Fundamentals 7-12 equal Value 2, etc. We're saying that, as a group, the Fundamentals are how we demonstrate our values in action. This allows us to focus fully on the Fundamentals, without having to "cancel out" the previous work we may have done. This approach has worked fabulously well every time.

Vision, mission, values

In this chapter, I've explained how values and behaviors are different, and why defining your culture in terms of behaviors is ultimately more useful. We've also taken a close look at how to go about defining those behaviors for maximum effectiveness. While my experience working with companies across the country in virtually every industry has shown me just how practical this approach is, I'd be remiss if I didn't also touch on how the Fundamentals System relates to the more traditional method of defining culture in terms of a vision, mission, and a set of core values. So let's do that now.

Vision

Almost every company, at some point, has done an exercise where they attempt to provide organizational clarity by defining a vision, mission, and set of core values. A vision statement is a description of some future state that you want to achieve. It strives to answer the question, "*Where* are we going?" It's typically aspirational and puts a "stake in the ground" as to where you want to be five or ten years from now. This might include statements like:

- We will exceed $100M in sales by 2025
- We will have the largest market share in our industry by the year 2022
- We will find a cure for breast cancer within seven years
- We will put a man on the moon by the end of the decade

The purpose of a good vision statement is to provide a clear, and ideally, inspiring goal for the organization. Being clear about where we're headed also helps the organization to make sound strategic decisions, since all decisions should help propel the organization toward its vision.

Mission

A mission statement is a statement of purpose. Its goal is to describe the reason the organization exists. It strives to answer the question, "*Why* do we do what we do?" Non-profit organizations almost always have a clear and compelling purpose, but most for-profit organizations also try to articulate a purpose. Beyond simply making money, is there some larger reason we exist? Here are some mission statements from large, well-known companies:

- To attract and attain customers with high-valued products and services and the most satisfying ownership experience in America. (Toyota)
- To bring inspiration and innovation to every athlete in the world. (Nike)
- To refresh the world, inspire moments of optimism and happiness, and to create value and make a difference. (Coke)
- To be the world's best quick-service restaurant experience. Being the best means providing outstanding quality, service, cleanliness, and value so that we make every customer in every restaurant smile. (McDonald's)

Core Values

Core values act as a set of high-level operating principles for the organization. They strive to answer the question, "*How* do we go about doing our business?" Most organizations will articulate between four and eight values. They may include ideas such as:

- Quality
- Service
- Innovation
- Integrity
- Teamwork
- Transparency
- Respect

Much has been written about the millennial generation and their desire to do work about which they can be passionate, and the quest to be part of something larger than themselves, to make a meaningful difference. In order to attract, retain, and inspire these folks, organizations of all types try to articulate a truly compelling vision, mission, and set of values. So what's wrong with any of this?

To be sure, nothing is wrong with the goal. Rather, it's the execution that's almost always sorely lacking. Instead of describing something that's authentic, they manufacture lofty statements that are so vague and generic that they fail to provide either clarity or inspiration. What's worse, they often generate cynicism and eye-rolls. Here are three actual mission statements taken from company websites:

- Our mission is to promptly respond to our client's needs for quality professional services through the effective management of our personnel resources, utilizing our extensive experience and knowledge while we remain strongly committed to innovation, partnership, and our client's interest.
- Our mission is to provide our customers with the highest quality people, products, and services needed for their success, while allowing for profitability and growth of the firm.
- Our mission is to provide the most technologically advanced products with responsive customer service. We strive to achieve a fair return for our suppliers and shareholders and a healthy, safe work environment for our Associates. We measure success by customer satisfaction, our industry reputation, a profitable business and the personal and professional growth of our Associates.

These statements are so broad that they provide almost no useful clarity. And they're certainly not likely to inspire anyone. Beyond their lack of utility, there's an even bigger danger: By the time the organization's leadership team finishes their work on drafting and polishing these statements, and puts them on their website and their walls, they think their work on culture is largely complete and they never take the next steps. The idea of culture is relegated to being intangible, lofty, amorphous, and not all that relevant to doing "real" work.

I'm obviously giving you examples here of how *not* to do this, and certainly there are organizations that do this work with great passion and authenticity. But my experience is that these are incredibly rare.

In the clouds or on the ground?

Rather than being lofty or impractical, defining "behaviors" as I've described them in this book is incredibly useful. People at all levels of the organization can relate to them. Behaviors are "on the ground" rather than being "in the clouds." They provide tremendous clarity about how we want to operate and what's expected.

To be absolutely clear here, I am not in any way against creating vision and mission statements. What I'm against are *vague and useless* vision and mission statements. My message to leaders is this: If you're not sure what your vision and mission are, keep thinking about them. Keep working on them. But don't put out statements that you don't believe in simply to be able to check the box and say you have them.

I'd rather see you begin by defining behaviors and then go back to work on your vision and mission. This way we can see real impact and applicability quickly. If instead we start with vision and mission, we run the risk of getting too frustrated and never going further.

When I was running RSI, I struggled with this issue for years. Every time I read a book about culture or went to a seminar, I was told that we had to have a compelling vision and mission. So I'd go home and try to come up with one, but everything I thought of felt forced and "fake" and I simply refused to put out something that wasn't authentic for me. Eventually, we did have a vision and mission, but it took a long time before I had enough clarity in my own mind to articulate them. In the meantime, though, we were crystal clear about our Fundamentals, and we had an incredibly aligned workforce.

In case you're wondering, our vision was

To be the best run small business in America

And our mission was

To help small and mid-size businesses to be more successful by making their benefits work, and by inspiring them through extraordinary service and performance excellence

The vision truly drove my efforts to optimize every single aspect of our business, from how we did sales to service to recruiting to finance to strategic planning. It had enormous influence over how we prioritized our activities.

The mission recognized that we were in the benefits business and that we were trying to help our clients be more successful, but it wasn't limited to benefits. We also wanted to inspire them to run their businesses better because of their interactions with us. It meant that doing seminars on best practices and sharing what we were doing with others wasn't a distraction; rather, it was a core part of our mission.

At High Performing Culture, we don't yet have a vision because I'm honestly not certain what our long-term goal is. Eventually I'll figure it out. Our mission, though, is

To transform people and organizations by providing them with the tools and the methodology to more consistently teach and practice the behaviors that drive success.

This mission is very real for us. The process we teach is truly transformational, and we each feel inspired by the opportunity to impact people and organizations so profoundly. The statement also describes, in simple terms, what we do to transform them.

Just like at RSI, we established our Fundamentals long before we crafted our mission statement. And while this may sound contrary to traditional thinking, my experience is that most of the time it's ultimately more practical.

Here's the bottom line: The first step to "institutionalizing" your culture is to define, with tremendous clarity, exactly what you want that culture to be. The fastest, most effective, most practical way to do this is to articulate the behaviors (Fundamentals) you want to see your people practicing. This enables you to truly operationalize your culture.

Once you've accomplished this successfully, you can always go back and work on your vision and mission to provide an even greater level of strategic clarity.

In the next chapter, we'll look at how to teach and practice your Fundamentals with the requisite consistency to ensure they become ingrained.

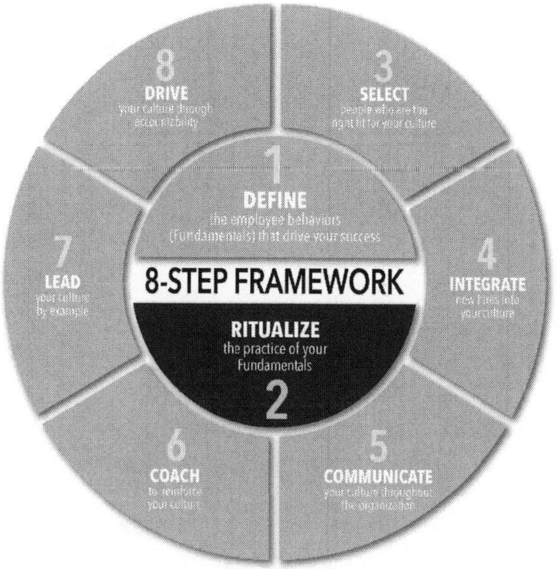

RITUALIZE the practice of your Fundamentals

I noted in Chapter 3 that creating rituals is one of the simplest and yet most powerful concepts I've ever learned. It truly is the key to helping us sustain our effort, and as a direct result, helping us to internalize the behaviors that drive success.

In this chapter, we'll take a close look at what I mean by "rituals," and I'll share with you some examples of rituals with which you're surely familiar. We'll explore why rituals are so important and how to avoid this initiative becoming the "flavor of the month." I'll also share with you the story of an event that literally changed the course of the rest of my career, and how I applied my learning from that event to create the original Fundamentals System at RSI. To make sure we can translate this concept into practical action, I'll provide you with examples of rituals that are particularly effective in the workplace, and some key learnings I've realized from working with so many organizations. Lastly, I'll share with you a simple way to understand and communicate the real power of rituals. We have a lot to do! Let's get started.

What is a ritual?

A "ritual," in the way that I use the term, is some behavior or practice that you do over and over again until it becomes a habit. Doing it becomes almost reflexive or second nature. It's just "one of those things we do around here."

Think about every time you go to a professional sporting event. What happens right before the opening kickoff of every NFL game, the first pitch of every MLB game, or the tipoff of every NBA game? The national anthem is played. It's not done only if we have enough time and can squeeze it in. It's not done only if someone remembers to do it. No; it happens every single time, without fail. It's a ritual. It's just what we do.

Imagine for a moment that it wasn't a ritual; that it was, in fact, only done when we we're not running behind schedule or when we have enough time. Do you think it would happen at every game? I doubt it. It might happen consistently for the first few weeks, but sooner or later we'd have a night or two when we couldn't fit it in. Then we'd begin to lose momentum, and we'd slowly stop doing it. But we don't leave it to chance. Instead, we have a ritual or a routine that we go through before every single game, and this ensures that the practice is sustained.

When I was a child, we recited the Pledge of Allegiance at the beginning of each school day. Many families begin every meal with a prayer. At every military funeral, buglers play Taps. These are rituals. They're not dependent on our discipline, our motivation, or our memory. They're just what we do.

Sticking with things

So why are rituals so important? Well, it's our nature as human beings that very few of us are good at sticking with things. In fact, we're pretty darn poor at it. How many times have you started a diet or exercise program, only to give it up after a few weeks or months? How many programs have we rolled out at work, determined to make this one last, only to see it forgotten or pushed aside when we got busy or when a new initiative took its place? No doubt we've all faced these challenges.

Throughout my career, I've worked with hundreds of entrepreneurial CEOs, and one thing many of them have in common is a certain degree of Attention Deficit Disorder. Of course, I don't mean this in a purely medical way, but rather that many of them have short attention spans, get distracted easily, and get very excited about new ideas. They think that as soon as they've understood a topic, it's essentially done. They don't have to actually *do* anything about it, do they? Once an idea gets to the implementation stage it gets pretty tedious and uninteresting, and before you know it, they've read another book or heard another speaker and want to implement something different. Does that sound familiar to you?

Well, rituals are what help us to stick with things when we wouldn't normally have the motivation or the discipline to do them ourselves. It's the ritual that keeps them going, not us.

A silly example

Let me share with you a rather silly example that I use all the time in my workshops. While it's a bit silly, I use it because it really helps to make this point clear. I'll be standing in front of a group of leaders and I'll ask them, "How many of you, when you woke up on Monday morning this week, said this to yourself: 'It's a brand new week, and this week I'm going to turn over a new leaf. I'm going to be incredibly focused, and really disciplined, and see if I can go every single day this week, and I mean *literally* every single day . . . brushing my teeth every morning.'" Not surprisingly, they all look at me quizzically, many of them laughing.

I'll feign as if I'm incredulous, "You mean, you *didn't* say that on Monday morning? So how many of you have managed to get it in every single day this week so far?" I'll ask. Of course, they all raise their hands, and when I ask them how they were able to pull this off, they quickly realize that it's because they have a ritual.

Most of us don't struggle to brush our teeth each morning. We don't debate with ourselves and have to somehow muster enough motivation to do it. No, instead, it's pretty much automatic. We typically have some set of activities that we do each morning that require almost no thought. We probably don't even remember doing them. It's just what we do. That's the power of a ritual! When something becomes a ritual, it's no longer difficult to do. It's just what we do.

So here's the key idea I'd like you to consider: If there was a way that we could create rituals that were as automatic as brushing our teeth, or doing the national anthem, around how we teach and practice those behaviors (Fundamentals) we wrote in the last chapter, it would be a virtual game changer! Now it would have a chance to last for years and years into the future because it wouldn't be dependent upon our ability or discipline or motivation to make it stick. It's the rituals that would keep it going, not us.

This is a topic we can't overpower with discipline and motivation. We can't say to ourselves, "I know I've never been all that disciplined before, but this time, I'm really going make it last." No, you're not. Even with the best of intentions, you're likely to get busy and distracted with other issues or initiatives. So if you're wise, you don't think that you're somehow going to show up with a level of discipline you've never shown before; instead, you build rituals and you *let the rituals do the work*.

Shortly, I'll show you just how to do that. But first, let me share with you the story of how I learned all this. I shared this in *Fundamentally Different*, but it's an important enough story that it bears repeating here and I think you'll see how it anchors these ideas.

The Ritz-Carlton

This story dates back to 2003. Our company, RSI, was always known for extraordinary customer service, and yet, I was constantly thinking about ways we could be even better. I decided to plan some activity to help us think bigger about how to deliver truly amazing service. So we closed the office one Friday at noon, not telling our staff what we were going to do, only that we'd be doing some offsite activity. Here's what we did.

I chartered a couple of buses and these buses pulled up to our office in southern NJ. Everyone came out of the office and climbed aboard the buses, no doubt curious about where we were going and what we were going to do. We drove from our office over to Center City, Philadelphia, and we went to the Ritz-Carlton. Our plan was to have lunch there, and then to spend the afternoon in a meeting room doing some brainstorming about fabulous customer service experiences. As you might imagine, the reason I chose to go there was to soak up "Ritz-Carlton-ness," if there is such a word; and I figured that if we went to the Red Roof Inn, we'd think Red Roof Inn-level thoughts, but if we went to a Ritz-Carlton, we'd think Ritz-Carlton-level thoughts!

Back in 2003, I didn't really know much about Ritz-Carlton, other than that they had a reputation for amazing customer service. While I didn't know for sure, I was guessing that it couldn't have been by accident. Rather, there must be systems and processes behind the scenes that enabled them to deliver their brand of service with such consistency. It couldn't be that they just hired nice people and it all just worked out on its own!

So I called my contact there and I explained my goals for the day. I asked if they could have someone come during lunch and spend a little time sharing with us some of those behind-the-scenes practices that drive their success. Not surprisingly, they readily agreed. They had a woman from their HR department spend about 20-25 minutes with us during lunch, and she shared with us two things that day that truly changed the course of the rest of my career.

The Basics

The first thing I learned is what's known as the Ritz-Carlton Basics. The Basics are 20 behaviors that describe how Ritz-Carlton delivers service. For example, "Escort guests rather than pointing out directions to another area of the hotel" or "Any employee who hears a customer complaint owns the complaint."

These Basics are numbered 1 through 20 and they're printed on a laminated card that all team members carry with them. I thought this was fascinating, but the more important thing is what they *do* with these Basics.

The Daily Line-up

Here's what happens. Every single day, in every Ritz-Carlton property around the world, in every department and in every shift, the team members get together at the beginning of the shift and they have a brief ten- to twelve-minute meeting known as the Daily Line-up. The first thing that happens in the Daily Line-up each day is that they spend a few minutes talking about the Basic of the Day. The rest of the brief meeting is spent on whatever is most relevant in that department that day, but it always begins with the Basic of the Day.

The Basics are reviewed like this each day, in order, until they get to #20, after which they go back to the beginning and do it again and again, every day throughout every team member's career. So in a given property, this may happen 30 or 40 times or more per day, given all the different departments and all the different shifts. And if today is day #14, it's day #14 in every Ritz-Carlton property in the world! Think about how powerful this is. They have more than 40,000 employees working in more than 30 different countries, and each one of them is in a Daily Line-up today talking about the exact same Basic. That's how you drive real consistency!

I learned all this that day back in 2003, and it got me thinking about why that works so well, and more importantly, how we could apply these same concepts in our company. Though we obviously weren't a hotel, the principles behind the idea were very powerful and had to be universally applicable.

Applying the concept

Fascinated, I went home that night and began to think about my own Basics. What were the behaviors that were most important to me and to us at RSI? Some I had written years before, but others were things I always said but had never actually codified anywhere. Over the course of a weekend I wrote out 30 behaviors that I wanted us to focus on and practice. I shared the list with my management team for their input, and I played with it and polished it for a few weeks until I felt it was ready to publish.

One of the first decisions I made was that these needed a name. I thought these were "fundamental" to our success, and so I decided to call them our "Fundamentals." We created a wallet-size card to easily carry and show them, along with a variety of other printed materials. And this is where the Fundamentals came from.

Well, it was great to write them down, but it was the Daily Line-up that really drove the adoption of the Basics at Ritz-Carlton. How could I do something similar at RSI? Our work environment wasn't anything like a hotel. Though we had departments, we didn't work in shifts and many of our people weren't even in the office every day, so I didn't think the Daily Line-up would work for us. Instead, I decided that we would focus on one Fundamental each week, and that throughout the week, we would do several different rituals to help us to think about, talk about, teach, practice, and focus on that week's Fundamental.

The Fundamental of the Week (FOW)

There were two rituals that I created when we first rolled out our Fundamentals at RSI, and we continue to practice these at High Performing Culture today. Because they work so well, most of our clients tend to do these two as well, and I certainly recommend them to everyone. In addition, there's a third ritual that I created a little more than three years ago, and we and most clients also do this one.

The first ritual I started at RSI was a weekly lesson delivered by e-mail and voicemail. Each Monday morning, I would send a message to the entire staff with the Fundamental of the Week (FOW) and a brief lesson that I wanted to share. The lesson might include a personal story or a recent example or whatever I wanted people to understand about the essence of the Fundamental. The lesson would typically be just a few paragraphs in length, and I sent it by e-mail and voicemail because some people prefer to read and some prefer to listen. A sample e-mail is included in Appendix C of this book. I did this for 30 consecutive weeks, or what I call the first "round."

When I finished the first round, I passed the baton to my senior leadership team, and I asked each member of the team to take a turn at sharing their thoughts about the week's Fundamental, and this continued for the next round of 30 weeks. As you might imagine, I wanted this to cascade throughout the organization rather than simply being the "David Friedman story."

When we finished the second round, I put a sign-up sheet in our kitchen and I asked the rest of our staff to pick a week that they wanted to be responsible for sharing the message of the week, from their own perspective, with their peers. And for years after that, at the start of every single week, a message would go out from the receptionist or a bookkeeper or a salesperson—literally, anyone in the organization.

Nearly every one of our clients now does this. It's a very powerful ritual because it serves two key purposes. First, it gives the CEO a chance to teach; to share his perspective on the Fundamental and why it's so important. Second, the "cascading" nature of the ritual creates a wonderful opportunity to transfer ownership to the rest of the staff. As an employee in an organization, I may find value in what the CEO has to say, but when I have to talk or write about it myself, I own it in a profoundly different and more impactful way. I watched this at RSI and I've seen it in company after company. When employees take over the weekly messages, a profound shift in ownership of the Fundamentals always takes place. Incidentally, many of our clients share with me the e-mails that their employees write, and consistently, the employees put an incredible amount of thoughts and effort into their messages.

> **The Fundamentals In Action**
>
> Berger Rental Communities is an award-winning property management company headquartered in Southeastern PA. A 2nd-generation family business with more than 180 team members, managing over 6,500 residential units, they've been practicing their Fundamentals since late 2012. In 2017, Berger was named the best property management company for eastern and central PA, NJ, DE, and MD.
>
> Observes Dan Berger, the CEO, "We're in the apartment management business. However, our success is really driven by our people, *not* our apartments. And that all starts with our intentional culture. Since we operate out of 24 different locations, I can't possibly visit them all with any frequency. So the only way we can create a consistent culture across all locations is by practicing our Fundamentals every week. Nothing is more important than our culture."

This is their chance to shine in front of their peers, and they take on that challenge and opportunity with great gusto.

Hedging the bet

I'm sometimes asked about whether we should screen or approve messages before they go out. While I don't think there's anything wrong with doing so, I've always chosen not to. There's, of course, a delicate balance between wanting employees to say what the Fundamental means to them and the risk that what they say totally misses the mark. I lean toward giving people a great deal of freedom to express themselves however they'd like. Having said that, there were a few things I always did to "hedge the bet" and increase the likelihood that the message would be on point.

First, I copied and pasted all my original e-mails onto one Word document and shared it with people so that, as they sat down to write, they could at least have my own message in their mind as a reference point. Second, when it was time for a new round of 30, I would gather all those who had signed up and provide a brief 20-minute training session with tips and suggestions. Third, every few years I would take a new round and write them myself. I thought of it as my way to "true" us up back to center in case we started to see too much drift away from my original intent.

In Appendix D, I've included some tips and suggestions for making this ritual more effective.

The first agenda item in meetings

The second ritual I created, patterned after the Ritz-Carlton Daily Line-up, is that we began every meeting with a brief discussion of the Fundamental of the Week. Unlike the Ritz, though, we didn't create a separate meeting for this purpose. Rather, we just used those times when we were meeting anyway and leveraged the opportunity to discuss the FOW. This would happen whether it was a management team meeting, a project team meeting, a department meeting, or even a customer meeting. If we had a meeting, we started with the FOW.

> **The Fundamentals In Action**
>
> "While it may sound strange at first, we talk about our 'Fieldamentals' in every customer meeting. It's amazing how often our Fieldamental of the Week just happens to fit perfectly with something that's important to that customer or prospect. And it helps them to see us in an entirely different light than other suppliers or service providers." – Jim Derry, CEO of Field Fastener

Nearly every one of our clients employs this ritual as well. The most effective way to do this is to have the leader engage the participants in a brief discussion by asking a question or two to get the dialogue started. I usually suggest that the leader of the meeting facilitate that discussion, but over time, it's even more impactful to rotate who's leading the discussion to get even greater engagement.

These discussions almost always help people to see new perspectives on the Fundamental and to notice additional ways that the Fundamental applies in their daily lives. This is where the nuance or the subtleties in the Fundamentals come to life. In fact, no matter how beautifully we wrote their descriptions, they can never stand alone. They only have meaning in the context of real life.

Written law vs. case law

In the legal profession, there's an important distinction made between what's known as the "written law" and what's called "case law." The written law refers to the actual statute. However, an entire body of additional interpretation is provided by judicial opinions written in response to real cases where the law must be applied. You can think of the regular discussion of the Fundamentals in a very similar way.

> **The Fundamentals In Action**
>
> Mike Mendiburu is the CEO of HighPoint, a global IT provider headquartered in NJ. When talking about building great business partner relationships, Mike says, "What we do is important, but *who we are is critical.* In any partnership, unforeseen circumstances will arise. Our partners need to know specifically how we'll respond in those situations. Our Fundamentals provide the answer. It's why we talk about our Fundamentals with every customer and with every business partner. The HighPoint Way defines who we are."

The original description of the Fundamental is the "written law." But all the dialogue and discussion around the Fundamental and how it applies is what forms the body of "case law." For example, one of my Fundamentals is to "Do the right thing, always." As simple as that may sound, in real life it's not so black and white. What's right for one may not always be what's right for another. Sometimes Fundamentals may even seem to conflict with each other. How do we apply good judgment in these situations? The daily discussions around the FOW provide a regular forum to explore these issues and evolve a deeper understanding of how to apply the Fundamental in day-to-day situations.

Episodic vs. systematic

This ritual is particularly powerful because it shifts our teaching from being "episodic" to being "systematic." If our teaching is episodic, it means that the only time I get to teach about this principle is when a situation arises. If this week's Fundamental is "Honor commitments," I may or may not see an incident where we failed to honor a commitment or perhaps went to great lengths to honor one. In the absence of these instances, when would I have the chance to teach anything about the Fundamental?

By employing this second ritual, we're creating multiple opportunities to talk about the Fundamental throughout the week. You may be in many different meetings this week, and in every one of them we're going to talk about what it means to "honor commitments." We're not limited by having to wait for an incident to arise. Instead, we're systematically talking about it throughout the entire week.

By the way, for those who wonder if it's hard to get in the habit of doing this, it really isn't. It's like saying a prayer before a meal or doing the national anthem before a ballgame. But there are some suggestions that can make establishing the ritual easier. Here are two easy ones.

Ideally, every meeting should have a written agenda. If you create a template for meeting agendas that everyone uses, you simply make the first item on the template the FOW. That's pretty easy.

Here's a bit of a silly idea, but it's very effective. You make a new rule that if a meeting starts and the leader of the meeting forgets to begin with the FOW, he owes everyone in the meeting a dollar. Do this once or twice, and everyone will remember! It's a little silly, but it definitely works.

In Appendix E, I've included some tips and suggestions for how to get the most out of this ritual.

eMinder™

The third ritual that most of our clients practice makes use of a proprietary software tool known as eMinder™. When I built eMinder, I was trying to solve three challenges:

1. How can we keep employees engaged in a way that doesn't take a lot of time?
2. How can we help employers keep focused in a way that doesn't take a lot of time?
3. How can we provide some measurement and accountability around the Fundamentals?

eMinder became the answer. Here's how it works: Each week on Monday morning, all employees receive an e-mail that simply reminds them of the FOW. On Wednesday morning, they receive another e-mail with a scenario-based lesson related to this week's Fundamental. In other words, it gives them a situation to consider where they have to apply the Fundamental and choose the best response among four possible alternatives. Once the employee chooses their response, they immediately get an e-mail that provides feedback. The feedback is different for each of the four responses, and includes an explanation of what would be the best answer and why.

If an employee doesn't respond Wednesday, she gets a reminder on Thursday. And if she doesn't respond on Thursday, she gets a final reminder on Friday. At the end of the week, the leaders can run reports by person, by location, or by department, in any date range, to assess how employees are doing in terms of participation as well as in answering the questions correctly.

Because it's multiple choice and it's only one question, it doesn't take much longer than a minute or two to participate. But it does force all employees to engage with the Fundamental every week, to apply their understanding to a real situation, and to get some useful feedback. It also spurs healthy discussion when they have questions about a scenario or disagree with a particular answer.

> **The Fundamentals In Action**
>
> eMinder has become an invaluable tool for setting clear expectations, according to Kathy Trahan, the CEO of Alliance Safety Council. Alliance, headquartered in Baton Rouge, LA, is a non-profit training and education company that provides safety and workforce development services to employers across the country.
>
> At the end of each week, Kathy runs reports to identify those employees who answered the eMinder question incorrectly and meets with each person individually—not to scold them, but to speak with them, to understand them better, and to make sure they're clear on her expectations about the best way to handle different situations. "I have to take personal responsibility and ownership for making sure everyone understands exactly what I mean by each of our Fundamentals," notes Kathy. With roughly 100 associates, Alliance typically runs between 95% and 100% participation each week.

There are other rituals that companies practice, and you have to choose ones that make sense for your organization and the way in which you work. I share these three here because they're the ones that I and most of our clients do, and they've been proven to be effective. Most importantly, I share them to give you a clearer understanding of what I mean by rituals, and to help you begin to think about how you might apply this pivotal concept in your organization.

Three key lessons

I'd like to share with you three key lessons that I've learned over time about rituals.

The power of cyclical rituals

The first lesson I've learned is the power and importance of what I call "cyclical" rituals. Cyclical rituals are ones in which we have a finite list of items and we go through them one at a time, in order, until we get to the end, at which point we go back to the beginning and do it over and over again. Doing the national anthem or brushing our teeth are rituals, but they're not cyclical rituals. Think of the way Ritz-Carlton practices their Basics 1-20 and then goes back to the beginning, or the way I practice my Fundamentals 1-30 and then go back to the beginning. These are cyclical rituals.

> **The Fundamentals In Action**
>
> As a manufacturing company with 900 employees working in eight locations, Pioneer Metal Finishing doesn't have the luxury of regular meetings, nor do all their employees have a company e-mail address. That doesn't stop them from focusing on their FOW, however. Says Shelly Gagen-Block, VP of HR and OD, "We have pre-shift huddles every day in our plants. On Mondays, shift leaders print the FOW e-mail and discuss it with their team. On Wednesdays, they print the eMinder question, debating the best answer and why. On the other days, they look for examples and stories to share that relate to the FOW. In some form or another, the Fundamental is part of every huddle."

The reason that cyclical rituals are so important really goes to how we learn and absorb information. If we were like most companies, and we unveiled our six core values and asked our people to practice six things at once, I think it would be too much to process and to think about. But imagine that if instead, we said this week, we're going to focus on just one thing. All week, we're going to talk about it, explore it, practice it, and tune up our awareness about it. Do you think we'd learn it better if we did this? Of course we would!

Because we're only focusing on one idea at a time, we're going to get much deeper learning and penetration. But because we're also going to cycle through them over and over, we get the best of both worlds. We get the increased learning that comes from the intensity of focus, but we also get exposed to all of them because we're going to keep cycling through them.

And this is why I said earlier that the number of Fundamentals doesn't really matter! Regardless of the number, we're only going to focus on one at a time. And we're going to keep doing them every week for the rest of our lives. So, whether you have 9 or 14 or 27 doesn't make much difference. Of course, there is some outer limit. If you had 400 of them, we'd never get back to the beginning. But outside of the extreme, it turns out that the number just isn't that big of a deal.

Remember, too, that we're not asking our people to memorize or recite these. We're not stopping them in the hallway and quizzing them. We just know that if we take one at a time, and we keep practicing them week after week after week, sooner or later they're going to become internalized. And that's the real goal.

Leveraging existing rituals

The second lesson I've learned about rituals is the importance of leveraging existing rituals wherever possible. The more effort you have to put into creating new routines, the more difficult it becomes to sustain them because you're fighting against years of old habits. However, almost all organizations already have rituals they've built into how they operate, even though they don't necessarily call them "rituals." Every Tuesday morning is a leadership meeting. Every Friday afternoon is a sales call. Many companies do daily "huddles," and many do safety rituals. Look for ways to work the Fundamentals into these existing rituals whenever you can.

Notice that in my company I didn't create a new meeting where we could discuss the FOW. Rather, we just took a few minutes of the meeting we were *already in* and used that as a chance to discuss the Fundamental. That doesn't take any extra time. We're already there anyway!

One of my favorite examples of rituals and the ease of leveraging existing ones is related to safety practices. Most companies I've worked with who are in construction or manufacturing industries practice some kinds of safety rituals. They may get together at the beginning of every day and review a safety topic or they may meet weekly to discuss safety. These are often called "toolbox talks." If you do a toolbox talk every week, I'd recommend just adding four or five minutes to your talk to discuss the FOW. If you do daily safety briefings, you might consider adding a few minutes to the Monday briefing and including the FOW. You already have the ritual in place. Just fold the Fundamental right into it.

Incidentally, when I ask these companies if it's hard to remember to do their safety discussion, they look at me incredulously. "No, that's just what we do," they'll say. That's what rituals are all about.

To take this example one step further, imagine we're comparing the safety record of two companies, A & B. Company A discusses safety every single morning in their toolbox talk while Company B simply posts a sign on the wall that says, "Be safe." Which one do you think is more likely to have a better safety record? No doubt, the first one.

Of course, the same is true of our culture. We can either post a sign on the wall with our vision, mission, and values, or we can practice it and work at it every day. Obviously, the latter is going to have far more impact.

Going back to our safety example for just a moment, imagine you work in a company where you practice safety rituals every day. You're painting your child's bedroom one weekend and you're trying to reach a difficult part of the ceiling. You're tempted to reach too far from your ladder to maintain good balance, but it takes too much time to get down and move the ladder. What are you likely to do? I suspect that you'll move the ladder so that you can reach the area safely. Safety has been so drilled into your brain that you likely can't help but to see potential hazards, and their remedies, everywhere you look. Well, the exact same thing happens with Fundamentals. When we talk about them every day, they eventually become embedded in our consciousness. We begin to see the world through the lens of our Fundamentals. That's how and when they become "institutionalized."

Creating interactivity

The third key lesson I've learned about rituals is the importance of creating engagement or interactivity to keep them fresh. For many organizations starting down this path, one of their biggest concerns is the fear that their rituals may become stale and meaningless over time, and that they'll simply be going through the motions and lose the intended impact. The key to avoiding this trap is to look for ways to create engagement.

Consider the ritual of starting all meetings with the FOW. If I simply stand in the front of the room and lecture about this week's Fundamental, and you're in a completely passive role, we increase the risk that the message will begin to go in one ear and out the other. But if I ask you questions and get you to participate in a discussion, then the message is far more likely to stay alive. Your brain is active. You're thinking. You're engaged. The more you can engage your people, the more meaningful the rituals will be, and the more imbedded they'll become.

> **The Fundamentals In Action**
>
> Festival Foods, a 31-location grocery store chain in Wisconsin, uses an interactive "gaming" platform to engage its 8,000 associates. Every day, at some point in their shift, each associate logs into an online tool known as "The Hub." Using iPads stationed in break areas, associates answer several questions that test their understanding of the Boomerang Basics (that's what they call their Fundamentals) as well as role-specific knowledge. The tool keeps score, is fun and interactive, and even allows associates to compete with or challenge others. By making it engaging, Festival Foods has been able to maintain the consistency of the ritual without losing its effectiveness.

I noted earlier that it's great to rotate who writes the message of the week and similarly, that it's very powerful to rotate who leads a discussion. These are ways of increasing engagement and keeping the ritual relevant. Another good way to keep it meaningful is to use personal stories and/or to weave in examples from customer situations. Stories have a way of capturing people's attention and helping them to see the relevance. These are far more engaging than a theoretical or conceptual discussion of the Fundamental.

The value of repetition

In the workshops that I do, I like to distill the essence of this entire concept of rituals into one very simple illustration. Let me share it with you here.

If you want to learn anything so well that you've totally mastered it or internalized it, whether you're trying to learn to be a great piano player, or you want to learn to speak a new language fluently, or you want to become a world-class tennis player, what's the most important thing you need to do? Practice, or repetition, of course!

I could spend all day explaining to you how to play the piano, but that's obviously not going to make you a great piano player. Instead, you're going to have to spend thousands of hours practicing so that it becomes almost second nature to you. And the same is true for virtually anything we want to master. In Malcolm Gladwell's bestseller, *Outliers*, he

> **The Fundamentals In Action**
>
> Zonatherm and ThermFlo, two Chicago-based sister companies who sell and service mission-critical power and cooling products, have been practicing their Fundamentals since 2014. For their 100+ employees, living the Fundamentals is just part of their daily experience. It's also part of their recognition program, called "High Five."
>
> Explains CEO Steve Izzo, "Whenever an employee sees a Fundamental in action, she goes to our 'High Five Board' and selects a card that corresponds to that Fundamental. She completes the card with a meaningful acknowledgment, identifying the specific action a teammate took, and the impact that action had. The cards are collected in a bowl, and at the end of the week, one card is selected as the winner. The winner gets to spin a wheel which determines the prize she wins. Of course, all the acknowledgments are then distributed to the appropriate employees, and they can even be redeemed for small cash awards as well. It's been a fun way to keep everyone focused on practicing our Fundamentals.

notes that it takes roughly 10,000 hours of repetition to achieve a level of mastery. According to Gladwell's research, this seems to be a common denominator across a wide variety of disciplines, whether that 10,000 hours is done in a few years or is spread across a lifetime. And while we could argue about whether the number is really 8,000 or 10,000 or 12,000, there's no question that repetition is the key to mastering something.

So, if we can agree upon that premise, that repetition is the key to internalizing something, then here's the big question for you: How many people do you know who *love* to do repetition? In my experience, the answer is "very few." For sure, there are some; but most people hate repetition. We get bored and distracted. We want to move on to something else. How many times have we tried to stick to the diet or exercise program or the initiative at work? Sooner or later it gets tedious and we quit. That's just human nature.

Well, if repetition is the key to internalizing something, but most people hate repetition, that would seem to be a pretty big problem! So, what's the key to doing repetition? Hint: it's not trying to make it fun or creating more variety or just trying to be more disciplined. Not that there's anything wrong with making it fun or creating variety. These are certainly helpful, but there are only so many ways to make practicing scales on the piano fun. No, *the key to successful, ongoing repetition is ritual.*

Once something becomes a ritual, or a habit, it's no longer difficult to maintain. It's just what we do. Think about the national anthem or brushing your teeth or the daily toolbox talk or the Basic of the Day or the Fundamental of the Week. It's virtually automatic. Again, it's just what we do. So, rituals are the key to keeping the repetition going and the repetition is the key to internalizing anything.

Now let's apply this basic thinking very directly to our culture. If institutionalizing our culture is nothing more than getting all our people to internalize the behaviors that drive success, they're not going to internalize them simply because we held a big company meeting and announced them. Nor are they going to internalize the behaviors because we put them in performance reviews or because we put posters on the walls. No, the only way our people will ever internalize those behaviors is when we teach them over and over and over again. And the only way we'll ever teach them with that much consistency, without getting bored, distracted, and quitting, is when we create rituals around them. That's why rituals are so foundational to success!

The chicken or the egg?

Of course, there is a little bit of a "Which comes first, the chicken or the egg?" aspect to this concept. In other words, it's easy to keep our practice going once we've formed a ritual or habit, but don't we have to do something long enough for it to become a habit in the first place? There's definitely some truth to this argument. It does take time for a habit to form, but there are things we can do to increase the odds of the habit taking hold.

For example, if we want to get in the habit of exercising every day, we're more likely to be successful if we work out at the same time each day or if we have friends that we meet at the gym every morning, than if we simply try to squeeze it in when we get a chance. I noted earlier that creating a meeting agenda template with the FOW as the first item is an easy way to help establish the habit of starting all meetings this way. This is also one of the reasons I suggest you look first to leverage rituals that already exist. The more we can make it easy to do, the more likely the habit will become established, and once established, it becomes quite easy to sustain.

Rituals vs. discipline

Contrary to what some might think, practicing rituals does *not* take discipline. In fact, to a certain extent, rituals replace the need for discipline. Let me explain.

Put simply, discipline is the ability to get yourself to do what you know you should do when you don't feel like doing it. When you don't feel like practicing, what's your inner dialogue that gets you to do it anyway? It takes a lot of psychic energy to wage that inner battle and overcome the tendency to take the easy way out. And given how much energy it takes, it's not likely to be sustainable. Very few people have the internal fortitude and discipline to stay with it over a long period of time. Eventually, we give in and sink back to our old habits.

Remember that when something becomes a ritual though, it's no longer hard to do. We don't have an inner battle, and it doesn't take discipline to brush our teeth. We just do it. This is why rituals or habits are much more reliable than discipline.

We never stop

As you'll learn more about in Chapter 11, we recommend doing annual surveys to hold yourself accountable and to measure progress on your performance in living to your Fundamentals. In the comments section of these surveys, I'll occasionally read a comment that looks something like this:

> "We've been practicing these Fundamentals for a year now. I think we all understand them. How long do we have to keep doing this?"

Here's my simple answer to that question: Do you think Michael Jordan stopped practicing free throws after he made it to the NBA or after he won his first championship? No, this is something we *never* stop practicing. And the more we practice, the better we get, the more we begin to see levels of depth and nuance we hadn't noticed before, and the more ingrained the Fundamentals become. After all, isn't that the ultimate goal?

In its simplest form, the Fundamentals System is a methodology to institutionalize our culture by clearly articulating the behaviors (Fundamentals) that drive success and then teaching and practicing them over and over again (through rituals) so that they become internalized. That's why these two steps are at the center of the 8-Step Framework.

Now that we understand the core of the framework, it's time to move to Step 3. In the next chapter, we'll take a closer look at how we can get better at selecting people who will be a good fit in the culture we're trying to create.

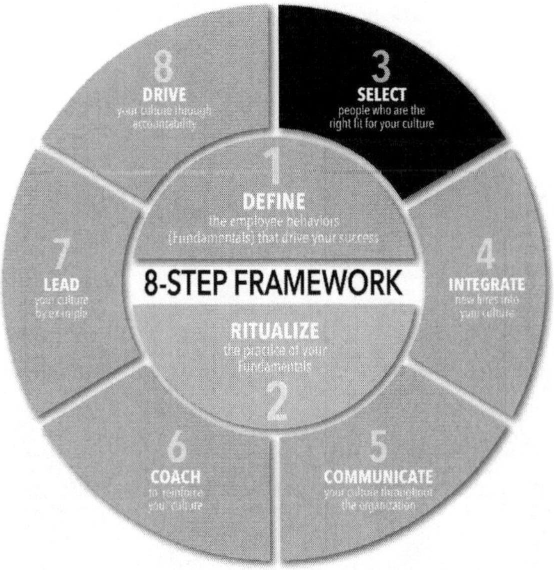

SELECT people who are the right fit for your culture

You can't bake a high-quality cake if you don't start with the best ingredients. The same is true with our organizations. It's virtually impossible to build a truly high-performing culture if we have too many people who don't fit that culture. Instead, we constantly struggle, trying to get people aligned, trying to get them working together effectively, but we're destined to fall short. In this chapter, we'll take a closer look at the third step in our 8-Step Framework: How to select the right people for the culture we're trying to build.

I noted in Chapter 3 that people generally come to the workplace already "fully baked." In other words, they are who they are. While we can certainly teach them skills, the basis of their value system is largely completed by the time they show up at your door. Their family upbringing is typically the biggest influence on their values, and then they're also further shaped by their previous experiences, at work and at home.

You might be wondering how this meshes with my comments in earlier chapters about how the culture in an organization significantly impacts the way in which people perform. Can people change or can't they?

Here's the easiest way I can explain it. I can take a person who has a heart for service and, when put in an environment that teaches, nurtures, and celebrates amazing service, that trait will blossom. Put that same person in a different environment, and that trait may become somewhat submerged. But I can't take a person who just doesn't "get" service and turn them into a fanatical service provider, no matter what kind of environment I put them in. We must start with people who are predisposed to being a good fit in the culture we're trying to create.

Of course, this is easier said than done. People don't typically show up wearing a sign that says, "I'm a good cultural fit." It isn't always easy to tell, and to be sure, we're never going to bat 1.000 when it comes to selecting people. We *will* make mistakes from time to time. However, there are two very different types of hiring mistakes. One is excusable; the other is not.

Two types of mistakes

The first mistake is a failure to recognize the signs or to read the signals properly. This is not unusual, and it's one we'll never eliminate entirely. People aren't always easy to read. Sometimes we don't pick up on a sign, or we simply misjudge a person. An interview is a pretty artificial environment, and we don't always get to know the "real" person. They're on their best behavior and they're naturally trying to show us what we want to see. There are definitely things we can do to improve our success, and I'll share some of those later in this chapter, but we'll never be perfect.

The second mistake is meeting someone who we *know* isn't a good cultural fit, but hiring them anyway. This is the mistake we have to avoid, and it's totally within our control. Unfortunately, I see this mistake far more frequently than the first one.

Why would we hire someone we know isn't a good fit? There are a variety of common reasons. Sometimes we convince ourselves that the person possesses a skill that's important enough to us that we're willing to overlook the rest of the picture. Other times, we think we're going to be able to change them. The most common reason, however, is pure desperation! We're short-staffed in a certain department, we've been looking for some time and haven't been able to find the right person, and we're unwilling to keep looking. It's as if we're comparing them to an empty chair rather than comparing them to what we're really looking for. So we hire them and figure we'll just deal with it later. Six months later, we have to fire the person and clean up the messes that were created by our shortsightedness. And then, of course, we still have to redo the hire anyway! But in the moment, it just felt easier to hire them.

While it sounds so simple, it actually takes a tremendous amount of leadership discipline to avoid this mistake. In the theoretical world, it's easy. But in the real world, we *are* faced with these pressures and challenges. We *do* need to fill roles in order to complete projects or serve our customers. In spite of this, we need to maintain our discipline and refuse to bring in people we don't believe will be a good fit because we'll never build the kind of organization we want if we do.

The importance of clarity

So how do we go about determining whether a candidate will be a good fit? As obvious as it might sound, it starts with having enough clarity about the culture we're trying to build. This is one of the reasons the 8-Step Framework begins with defining your culture. The clearer you are about what you want your culture to be, the easier it will be to identify the right people. When we don't have that clarity, we're left with this vague sense that a person just doesn't "feel" right, or perhaps they do seem to feel right, but there's something we can't quite put our finger on. Even worse, if multiple people are involved in the interviewing process, and they each have a different notion of our culture because we haven't defined it clearly enough, there's likely to be a difference of opinion about the hiring decision and no concrete way to sort it out.

Before we go further, I want to be clear about two important points. First, when I talk about the importance of only hiring people who will be a good cultural fit, I'm not at all suggesting that it's OK to hire people who don't have the talent, skills, knowledge, or experience that you're looking for. I'm assuming you've found that; but in addition, the person has to also be a good cultural fit. It's not one or the other; it's both.

Second, saying that someone is or isn't a good fit has nothing to do with their gender, ethnicity, religion, or whether or not they're a good person. She may be a wonderful human being and we could be great friends, but that doesn't make her a good fit in the culture we're trying to build. This is about fit, not about judging a person's worth as a human or even as a friend.

By the way, it's also important to note that we're talking about hiring people who embody the culture we're trying to build, which may or may not be in line with the culture we have today.

Intrinsic vs. learned

Not surprisingly, the single best tool you have for assessing cultural fit is the interview. This is your chance to probe deeply and to get to know the candidate and what makes him tick. If you've developed a good set of Fundamentals, you can then write interview questions around the Fundamentals.

When you look at your Fundamentals, you'll find that you can break them down into two broad categories—those that are "intrinsic" and those that are "learned" behaviors. As the name would suggest, intrinsic ones are those that are part of someone's nature. They either have this quality or they don't. For example, one of my company's Fundamentals is "Deliver legendary service." As I noted earlier, I think some people really have a desire to serve, while others just seem to be missing the genetic code for service. I think it's intrinsic. Another intrinsic one for me is "Make quality personal." There are some people who have a tremendous passion for excellence. They just can't stand mediocrity in anything they do. For others, decent is good enough. It's doesn't matter to them whether or not a thing is done to the highest quality possible. Again, this doesn't make them bad people. They just wouldn't fit as well in a place where everyone is so passionate about quality.

Other Fundamentals tend to be learned behaviors. For example, "Practice blameless problem solving." Some people may have been brought up in families or worked in environments in which blame was a constant companion. Over time, they may have learned that blaming others is the way you survive in those environments. Assuming it hasn't become too deeply ingrained, we can teach them that we do things differently in our organization. Another example of a Fundamental that's more learned is "Get clear on expectations." I don't think people are born being good at setting and asking for expectations. It has to be taught.

Once you've divided your Fundamentals into intrinsic and learned ones, the next step is to write interview questions around the most important intrinsic ones for the position in question.

Writing good interview questions

When writing good interview questions, I try to follow three simple rules. First, I try to develop questions that ask the candidate to tell me stories or give me examples, rather than telling me what they "think" about something. For example, "Tell me about a time when you delivered amazing service to a customer. What was the situation and what did you do?" I'm not asking what she "thinks" about service or even what she theoretically would do in a hypothetical situation. I want to know what she actually *did.* As I listen, I'm looking for whether she gets it. I'm watching her body language. I'm noticing how animated she does or doesn't get. I'm getting a glimpse into where she really is about service.

My second rule is to ask open-ended questions rather than "yes/no" questions. Here again, the more I can get the person talking, the more I'm seeing how he looks at the world. For example, "Tell me about a project in your last job that you were most proud of. What did you do and why were you so proud?" Obviously, this would give me far more information than "Did you like your last job?"

Third, I try to develop questions that don't necessarily telegraph what I'm looking for. Let's suppose I'm looking for someone who prefers to work on teams, as one of our Fundamentals is to "Think team first." Rather than asking, "Do you like to work on teams?" I might use a question like the previous one where I asked about a project he was proud of. If the story he tells me is about a time in which he had total control over every aspect of a job and he loved it because he didn't have to depend on anyone, he might be a superstar, but chances are he's not likely to be a team player. If the story he chooses to tell me is about a time in which he worked on an interdisciplinary team and he loved how he gained new insights by seeing things from totally different perspectives, there's a higher probability he's going to be more team oriented.

> **The Fundamentals In Action**
>
> At Festival Foods, the Wisconsin grocer mentioned in the last chapter, finding team members who fit their unique culture is critical. To help ensure success in this effort, they've developed a bank of interview questions focused on their "Boomerang Basics."
>
> For each Basic, they have 3-4 behavioral interview questions that help get to the heart of whether or not a candidate will be a good fit. They even have a separate list for hourly workers and one for leadership so that questions are relevant for each category. Making sure that every associate is a good fit has helped Festival to maintain their culture, despite their significant growth.

Personality tests

I'm often asked about various assessment tools and their role in selecting people who are likely to be a good fit. There are many different tools available, from DiSC to Predictive Index to

Caliper to Myers-Briggs and others. At RSI, we used DiSC, though I don't have a strong preference for one over another.

Overall, I'm an advocate for using profiling instruments like these as I think they can provide important additional insights, but I'll offer two caveats. First, I think it's important to share the results with the candidate and use them as a discussion point. The candidate may agree or disagree with parts, may provide additional context or background, or perhaps she may even help you to see the results in a different light. If you see aspects in the report that give you concern, it's appropriate to be honest about that and see how the candidate responds. Remember, the goal is to get as much insight as possible into who this person really is.

My second caveat is that I never like to make decisions based solely on the report generated by one of these instruments. Rather, the report provides additional data points to be added to your interview, references, and any other information you collected. Again, the report is a data point, not the entire picture.

Person descriptions

Another tool that we've used effectively is to create a "person description" for each role. This is an idea I learned from one of my earliest mentors, Carter Schelling, and it can actually be used for any type of decision you're trying to make in a more objective way. A person description differs from a job description in that it's a list of the traits and characteristics the ideal person for the job should possess, rather than a list of the duties and responsibilities of the job. The key to how this tool is used is that you take 100 points and spread them among the various attributes. This forces you to give a relative prioritization to each. For example, if you had ten attributes and all were equally important, they would each get 10 points. However, one attribute might be truly be worth 60 of the available 100 points and another might only be worth 5.

Once you've distributed the points, you now have a scorecard you can use when evaluating candidates. This helps you to stay more grounded in what you said was most important, rather than being "seduced" by someone you really like but who doesn't have any of the attributes you were looking for.

Incidentally, since the scoring is still subjective, small differences in scoring are inconsequential. If one candidate scores 83 and another scores 85, I would regard those as essentially identical. However, if one scores 85 and another scores 65, that's a pretty significant difference in the degree of match between what you said you were looking for and what this candidate presents.

Other tools

Beyond the interview, profiling instrument, person description, and references, you can often get good feedback from your current staff with regard to a potential candidate's degree of cultural fit. Depending on the nature of the position, you might consider having some of your current team meet with the candidate or even go to lunch with her to see what insights they're able to garner. This may not be appropriate for every position, and it's important to give your team guidance on what you're looking for, otherwise it can be more confusing than helpful.

One final suggestion: It can be useful to assign a person on your staff, typically an HR professional, to be the advocate for your culture in the interview process. Sometimes the hiring manager, even with the best of intentions, is so eager to fill a role that he may be tempted to overlook a potential cultural problem.

In these cases, having someone serve as the strongest advocate for the culture can help to make sure that we don't overlook this piece of the picture. At RSI, the final decision always resided with the hiring manager, but my HR Director always made sure that culture played a significant role in the discussion.

What about existing employees?

So far, our discussion has been entirely focused on the process for selecting new people to add to our team. But what about some of the people you currently have who may not be such a good fit? You may have let these people in the door when you weren't being so rigorous about your culture, or perhaps you may even have inherited them. How do we handle these folks?

My experience is that when you begin to become more serious about your culture, and you assess your current staff in terms of their degree of cultural fit, you'll find that they tend to fall into three broad categories. (I realize that this is an oversimplified model, but I think it's largely true and is therefore useful.) The first category are those people who are a great fit for where you're taking your organization, and if you were considering them as potential new employees today, they'd make the cut. In a good company, you'll typically have 70-75% of your people in this category.

The second category comprises those people who aren't bad. They probably wouldn't make the cut if you were considering them as new candidates, but they do decent work and they don't make waves. Interestingly, some of them may have been a great fit at the time that you hired them, but the organization has changed and they haven't been able to change with it. Typically we find this group represents 20-25% of most workforces.

The third group comprises those people who are poisonous. They're subversive. They're actually hurting your company from within. Whenever you try to roll out a new initiative, they undermine it with their cynicism. In most companies, this represents 0-5% of the workforce.

My advice is to get rid of those in the third group as quickly as you can. They make it inordinately more difficult to move the organization to where you want to go. They're like a cancer that needs to be excised. No doubt you've seen this and know exactly what I'm referring to.

With the group in the middle, I would coach and mentor them as much as you can, but I wouldn't expect many of them to make it long-term. To be clear, some will be able to change, and they deserve that chance. Others are likely to drop out as they see the way in which the organization is changing.

As you become more and more rigorous about hiring only people who are a good fit, your percentage in the first category begins to shift from 75% to 80% to 85% and then to 90% or more. There becomes so much peer pressure in the right direction that the few remaining people who aren't a good fit tend to select themselves out. It becomes easier and easier to build what you want.

Shades of gray

Before we leave this discussion of selecting people who will be a good fit for your culture, I want to confess that I've made this sound much more "black and white" than it really is. Rarely are people simply a "good fit" or a "bad fit." More often, there are many shades of gray. To be sure, we may even be more willing to accept some people who aren't a perfect fit if they bring essential skills or experience. And the stronger your culture is, the more likely it will ultimately influence that person to behave in ways that better match your organizational norms. As with everything, it's a question of degree. Bringing in someone who is a lousy fit for your culture is a prescription for failure. The more rigorous we can be about selecting people who fit our culture, the more success we'll have in building a truly high-performing organization.

Once we've found these great people, how we integrate them into our culture is critical. And this is the focus of Chapter 7.

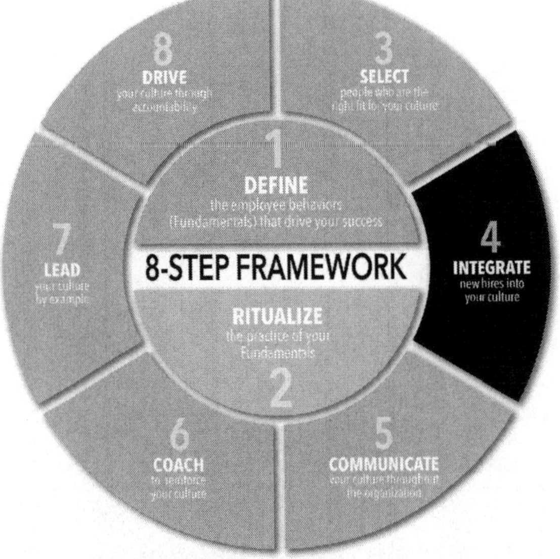

INTEGRATE new hires into your culture

Think about the last time you started in a new job. You probably felt a bit uncomfortable, even nervous, not really knowing what it would be like. What will be expected of me? Will I fit in? How will I ever learn the written and unwritten rules that govern the way things get done? You were like a sponge, trying to figure it all out.

If you've been at your company for many years, and especially if you're the CEO, you may not remember what's it's like to be new, and consequently, you may fail to appreciate just how impactful those early days are. I often say that the first week a new employee spends in your company is actually the most important week in their entire career. It's that impactful.

First impressions

This is the first impression new hires are getting of how the company functions. Are people friendly? Do they work as a team or is it "every man for himself"? Is leadership respected? Are people passionately engaged in the company's mission or just "punching the clock"? Do they have pride in their work or are they doing the minimum necessary to get by? These first impressions are typically imprinted in a powerful way, and they're difficult to change later.

And by the way, those first impressions actually start long before a person's first day of work. They start as soon as the person has any interaction with your organization, certainly with the interview at a minimum. What was the experience like when they applied for the job? How about when they were scheduling the

> **The Fundamentals In Action**
>
> The tagline for Northwestern Benefit Corp. of GA, an Atlanta-based employee benefits consulting company, is "Intentionally Different," and their difference is mostly driven by their culture. They've been practicing their Fundamentals (they call them "Tenets") for more than twelve years, and have grown in that time from a staff of 20 to now more than 130 professionals. Given that rapid growth, it's not surprising they place tremendous emphasis on how they integrate new employees into their culture.
>
> Their CEO, David Asbury, is intimately involved throughout integration. "It actually starts pre-integration," says David. "Before a person's first day of work, we send a book, our Tenets, a welcome letter, and even the integration schedule. On their first day, their workstation is set up, they have business cards, passwords, etc. I personally spend two hours with them on that first day, mostly focusing on our Tenets. We want to show new people from the very beginning just how serious we are about doing things right."

interview? Remember that they're a blank slate and every experience is creating an imprint.

Are you orchestrating every aspect of that experience to create the impression you want, or is it happening haphazardly? Too often it's the latter, and it has an enormous impact on your success in building the culture you want. In this chapter, we'll take a closer look at how you can build a world-class integration program that supports and deepens your culture by managing those early impressions and setting people up for success.

Writing the prescription

There's an analogy I like to use when thinking about the importance of orchestrating those early experiences. Imagine you're starting at our company and on your first day I hand you a pair of prescription glasses to wear. The glasses serve as a filter through which you see everything. I could hand you three different pairs of glasses with three different prescriptions, and if you looked at the same thing it would appear different based on which glasses you were wearing. The glasses influence your perception.

You have the ability to write the prescription for the glasses a new person puts on. They're going to see, hear, and experience a variety of things, and you can influence the interpretation they apply to those events. Done properly, you have an opportunity to shape their perceptions. In a sense, it's like brainwashing, but in a healthy, productive way. And if you don't take advantage of that opportunity at the very beginning, it's like allowing the new person to walk up to a pile of eyeglasses and randomly choose which ones to wear. And who knows what the prescription is or what they're seeing? Even worse, what if one of those cynical jerks I referred to earlier gets to the new person and gives her their glasses? Just think of the impact that would have.

Remember, as well, that these early impressions tend to be lasting. It's like a mold that at first is flexible and malleable, and over time it becomes hardened and more rigid. We tend to be the same way. Once we form our judgments and opinions, these views color our perception in a way that supports what we've come to believe. It's incredibly hard to undo this later. That's why it's so critical that we seize the opportunity to write that prescription as early as possible.

Integration

You may remember from my overview of the 8-Step Framework in Chapter 3 that I prefer to use the word "integration" vs. "orientation" or "onboarding" because I think the word carries with it a different connotation. It's a word of assimilation that conveys a sense that we're going to help you to become a part of who we are. I'll be using that word throughout this book, though you can of course use whatever word you prefer.

To be clear, as I talk about integration, I'm referring mostly to how new employees get inculcated into the organization. I'm generally not including their job-specific training in this definition, but rather how they learn all about the organization, its culture, what it does, and how it does it.

A long-term perspective

As you think about the investment in time and resources you're willing to devote to integration, it's important to view it from a long-term perspective. For example, let's assume for the sake of illustration that your integration process is one week long (yours may be shorter or longer). If you look at this from the perspective of the first month, you'd think, "That's crazy. We can't afford to lose 1/4 of the productive time available for this person!" But if you look at it from the perspective of a year, it's only 1/52 of the year, or less than 2% spent on integration. And if you look at this from the perspective of a five- or ten-year horizon, it would be virtually inconsequential. Think of someone you hired ten years ago and imagine that for the first week you didn't let her do any real work. You probably wouldn't even remember that fact, and yet, the impact of integrating her effectively would be felt throughout her entire career. That's what I mean when I say you have to think of your investment in integration from a long-term perspective.

Being uncompromising

I would also suggest that the consistency with which you approach integration should be "uncompromising." By uncompromising, I mean that every single employee goes through integration. This is the same kind of approach I advocate for selecting the right people for your team. Just as we don't want to ever bring in someone we don't believe is going to be a good fit, we also don't ever want to start someone without having him go through a proper integration.

Being uncompromising here also requires the same kind of leadership discipline I referred to in the selection process. There will always be times in which expediency challenges you to compromise. When a key manager suggests, "I know we usually like people to go through integration first, but we're really desperate to get this person online and productive, so how 'bout we skip it this time and just catch up on it later," you have to be the leader who keeps that long-term perspective in mind and insists that we bring the person in the "right way."

At RSI, all employees went through the exact same integration, whether they were a manager or a receptionist or a bookkeeper. Once they completed integration, they went to more job-specific training for their role, but the basic things they needed to learn about our company, and the way in which they learned them, were the same.

While that worked for RSI, I recognize that many organizations have people at vastly different pay levels and with vastly different levels of turnover. It may not make any sense at all to spend an entire week integrating someone who's a part-time, hourly worker in a high-turnover position. With that being said, the critical point is that you design an integration program that's appropriate for your workforce, and that you're consistent in having every new person go through that program.

In some companies, it may be entirely appropriate to have different integration programs for different people. Perhaps the full-time salaried employees have a one-week integration, the full-time hourly staff have a one-day integration, and the part-time staff have a two-hour integration. Again, the key issue is consistency. Every new person goes through the designated integration program before beginning to work. This discipline will pay big dividends not only in terms of the culture, but also in terms of their ultimate productivity.

I'll share with you in this section some of the elements of the RSI integration program simply to give you a sense of what a world-class program can look like. I should point out that what I'm describing didn't start that way. Rather, it was the result of years of iterations of improvement that came from a disciplined commitment to creating maximum impact. I offer it both as a source of inspiration as well as a source of some good ideas that you can apply. But while it's great to envision what it can eventually look like, it's equally important that I provide you with a blueprint for how to begin, no matter where you are, and how to build from there.

RSI Integration

At RSI, our integration began long before a person's first day of work. Every interaction that a potential candidate had with us, from speaking to our internal recruiter to coming in for an interview, was handled in a way that created the impression we wanted—namely that we were professional, friendly, helpful, and extraordinarily well-run.

Once a hiring decision was made, our HR director would give me the person's name, home address, and a little background information. I would then send a personal, hand-written note to the employee at home. It wasn't a form letter, and it wasn't something signed and sent by my executive assistant. It was a handwritten note from me. This was an important opportunity to demonstrate two of our Fundamentals: "Practice the 'human touch'" and "Create a feeling of friendliness and warmth in every interaction."

Several days later, the new person would get another piece of mail from me. This included our Fundamentals card and a personal note explaining what this was and asking them to review it before their first day. Several days later, yet another letter would arrive that included a one-page description of a group of five Fundamentals that were collectively known as "The Collaborative Way." And believe it or not, they'd get one last piece of mail from me before their first day! This was a CD that I recorded with a further description of our philosophy, as well as a bit about our differentiation.

When the new person showed up on the first day, there would be a mentor waiting to greet her, there would be a welcome sign in the reception area, her workstation would be ready with her nameplate, her business cards would be printed and at her desk, and there would be a welcome plant at her desk as well. There would also be an "integration binder" that included the complete schedule for integration as well as all the supporting documents, reading material, and homework assignments she would need throughout integration. The schedule detailed every hour, where she would be, with whom she would be meeting, and thc topic to be covered.

The length of our integration grew and shrunk many times over the years as we experimented with different ideas, but it typically ranged from about 5–8 days. During that time, the new person would meet with many different employees who would teach her everything from our strategy to our history to our differentiation to how we made money (we practiced Open Book Management) to what each department does to how to work the photocopy machine.

Every integration began with me on the first morning of the first day, as this was my best chance to "brainwash" people from the very outset. I spent two hours talking about our culture and our Fundamentals, demonstrating my passion for our culture. If we were trying to schedule an integration class and I wasn't available on the intended first day, we'd hold off their start until I was! It was that important to start people in the right way.

Given the amount of time and effort our entire organization put into how we brought in new members of the team, we always tried to group people together so that there would be an integration class of typically 3–5 people. We would simply speed up hiring in one department and slow it down in another so that we could make this work. Beyond the obvious efficiency from an organizational perspective, there's also a special bond that forms between employees going through a common experience, and they stay close to their integration "classmates" throughout their career.

On the last day of integration, the group would work together on the "RSI test." This was an open-book test that required them to answer a wide variety of questions that ranged from being able to explain our differentiation to knowing trivia about our employees. It was almost 20 pages of information and typically took 3–4 hours to complete. They would also complete a self-assessment that asked them to rate their understanding of a variety of topics on a 1–10 scale, as well as to provide feedback and suggestions for improvement. I should note that every single integration we did included some incremental improvement over the previous one based upon this feedback.

Below are some actual comments from employees' self-assessments. They give you a sense of just how impactful this process was:

- *"I was impressed by many things, but the most important was the company's culture. It is truly amazing how much effort is taken during the recruiting process to find employees who are the right cultural fit for RSI."*
- *"Any company can explain their vision, mission, and values, but I was impressed to find that the Fundamentals were actually practiced by all RSI employees."*
- *"I have been most impressed with the unified culture that has been promoted here. Everyone truly believes and adheres to this code, and that is extremely impressive."*

- *"The culture created within this organization is one I heard a great deal about during the interview process, but even still, I would never have imagined it being so real and complete."*
- *"I have been most impressed with RSI's culture and how each employee actually fits the culture. It is continually practiced by everyone, including the executive management, which I feel is very important."*

About 4–6 weeks post-integration, I also took the group to lunch. It was a chance for me to check in with them to see how things were going now that they were actually doing work. It was also a chance to get additional input about improvements we could make to better prepare them to be successful in our organization.

I could write an entire book just on integration, but I imagine by now you're getting a pretty good sense of what this was like and its impact on our people and our culture. What was happening in integration was actually happening on two concurrent levels. On one level was the foundational information they were learning to prepare them for success. In fact, after one week with us, they probably knew more about our company and our people than they knew in ten years at their previous company!

But on an entirely different level, think about the messages they were receiving about *how* we work. They were learning about planning and preparedness and details and execution. They were realizing that they'd joined a "major league" organization and that we play at an incredibly high level. And if we hired right, they were so excited about this. We hadn't let them do any work yet, and they'd be chomping at the bit, eager to prove to us that they're worthy of this opportunity! Note as well, that it would be rather incongruous of us to expect them to do high-quality work with our clients, but not be fully prepared for them. We need to show our people the same kind of focus and attention that we expect them to show to our clients.

Now compare this to how most of us begin our careers with a company. We show up on the first day and the company may or may not be prepared for us. We don't have business cards. Our phone isn't set up yet, but we're told that IT should get to us soon. We're whisked around and quickly introduced to some of the staff but can hardly remember their names by the end of the day. We spend half the day filling out HR paperwork and benefit enrollment forms. Does this sound familiar?

Companies spend so much time, effort, and money in recruiting, trying to identify and bring in the best people, but then so often fall woefully short in how they integrate these people. And then they wonder why it didn't work out. If they took just a fraction of those resources that were spent on hiring and dumped them back into integration, it would have an enormous impact.

How to begin

At this point you understand how important integration is and have at least a mental image of what it could ultimately grow to be. But that's not where you are now and you need to start somewhere. How do you begin?

The first thing I would tell you is that I'd rather you start small and be consistent than build the most amazing program that took so much time and effort that you stopped doing it after a few times. As I constantly repeat throughout this book, if we can't make it last, it's not worth doing.

There are three elements that *every* integration program should include. Let me explain them here.

Culture

As a new employee, somehow during integration I have to be *taught* the culture of this company. When I say taught, I mean that someone has to actually sit down and explain it to me, rather than having me try to figure it out on my own. The best person to do this is the CEO. No one can speak about it with as much passion and conviction as the CEO. If that's not feasible, because perhaps the employee works in a different location, then it should be the highest-ranking person who is available—perhaps a VP or a plant manager.

Beyond the passion that the CEO can demonstrate, there's also the symbolic significance that's communicated when it's done by the CEO. We're showing the new person just how serious we are and how committed we are to our culture.

This could be as simple as a 30-minute discussion, with the CEO talking about the Fundamentals and their importance and then highlighting a handful of her favorite ones. Over time, this can grow to a much more in-depth discussion that includes a variety of executives and other employees. It could eventually include an eLearning component, video training, and any number of other components. The key is that the culture has to be specifically taught to new people.

Context

The second thing I have to learn as a new employee is what I call "context." By context, I mean that the new employee has to learn how what he does fits into the larger picture of what your company does. If you simply put them in the corner and tell them to do their job, but they don't understand how it connects with the big picture, not only will it be less satisfying for the employee, but you'll also be limiting the extent to which they can make a meaningful contribution.

At RSI, this included learning our history, our strategy, how we differentiated ourselves, who we sold to, who our competitors were, how we made money, what each department did, etc. This helped people to feel a part of something larger and helped them to understand how they fit in.

Here again, this can start very small and doesn't have to be complex. In fact, it can be as simple as a 30-minute review of the organizational chart, explaining each department and their role, and perhaps highlighting the department in which the new person participates. Or for some, it might be some kind of linear chart that shows each of the steps in the value chain from sales to operations to finance, again highlighting the new person's role and explaining how her job connects to the people before her and after her.

This could grow in time to perhaps meeting with people in each department who explain their roles, or even spending time in those departments seeing what they do, or if appropriate, actually working in other departments. But it can start with as little as a brief overview with a chart and a highlighter. The point is that the better I understand my role, the greater my potential contribution will be.

Logistics

The third element that every integration program should include is what I call "logistics." By this, I mean the day-to-day mundane things people need to know in order to function in the organization. These are simple things like

- How do I work the photocopy machine?
- Who do I talk to if I need new business cards?
- Where do you get lunch around here?
- Who do I talk to if my computer breaks down?
- How do I work the voicemail system?
- What's the combination for the back door?
- Where do you get more toilet paper for the men's room?

As mundane as these topics are, we often fail to explain them to new people, and as a result, we slow the process of their becoming fully functioning, productive members of our team. The faster a new person starts to feel relaxed, comfortable, and confident, the sooner he'll be productive.

Here's the easiest way to address this topic: Go to the last five people you've hired and ask them one simple thing: "Name three things you wish people told you on the first day but they didn't." Then compile the list and make sure someone meets with the new people and explains everything on the list. Here again, we don't want to simply stuff the list in the new hire paperwork. Rather, we want to actually review these items with them.

Again, start small. Even if it's just a two-hour program, make sure you cover culture, context, and logistics, and make sure that every integration includes at least one iterative improvement from the previous one. If you do this, over time, you'll develop a truly world-class integration program, and more importantly, you'll begin to see the powerful impact it can have on your culture.

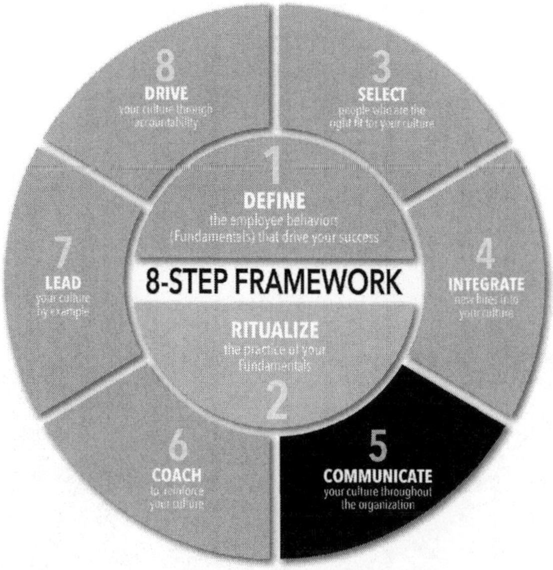

COMMUNICATE your culture throughout the organization

The company known as Successories has made a fortune producing and selling motivational posters, t-shirts, mugs, trophies, and virtually anything you can think of to promote positive behaviors in the workplace. At this point, they've become so popular that I'll bet nearly everyone reading this book has seen their images in one workplace or another. And while the thoughts they convey are no doubt inspiring, they've become so ubiquitous, even in lousy work environments, that many people have become jaded or cynical when it comes to displaying messages about their own culture. In fact, there's even a company called Despair, Inc. that's capitalized on this cynicism by creating hilarious posters, calendars, and other items with sayings to "de-motivate" people. They're actually quite funny.

To be sure, the issue isn't that we shouldn't be displaying our values, it's that too often we're displaying messages that are incongruent with the way people actually behave in our culture. We talk about teamwork, but then people work and think in silos. Or we talk about quality, but our people are forced to produce at warp speed and without the proper tools, such that the expectation of quality becomes a farce.

While displaying inspirational posters that run counter to reality is not going to somehow magically transform our culture, and may likely even create cynicism, that doesn't mean that consistent messaging is not important. If what we say about our culture *is* real and it's authentic and genuine, and people experience it daily, then the more I see it exhibited all around me, the better. If the only time your employees ever see a written form of your culture is on their first day, on an 8 1/2 x 11 piece of paper stuck in the new hire paperwork, sandwiched between the I-9 and the benefit enrollment forms, how likely are they to be thinking about it, talking about it, or having it seep into their consciousness? Not very!

As long as what you're displaying accurately reflects the culture you're genuinely working toward building, there's no limit to all the ways you can and should display your Fundamentals. And the more people see them, the more likely they're thinking and talking about them. Let me offer a few ideas in this chapter to spur your thinking.

Posters

At RSI, we had a beautifully framed poster of each of our 30 Fundamentals lining the hallways of our corporate office, each with a museum-type light fixture artfully focused on it. We've created similar wall art for many of our clients. Seeing these prominently displayed sends a strong message—to both your own staff as well as visitors—that this is important to you. If you don't have enough room (or the budget) to create individual posters, you can create a single poster that includes all of your Fundamentals on it. We've done this many times as well.

Electronic display boards

Many companies have electronic display boards in the reception area and/or throughout the facility. These display boards can be easily programmed to scroll through all the Fundamentals, or even better, to always show the week's Fundamental. While we didn't have an electronic display back in my RSI days, we did display the Fundamental of the Week on an easel in the reception area so that it was clearly visible to all visitors, and of course, was a reminder to our own staff as well.

Website

Most companies who are serious about their culture have some description of that culture on their website. Certainly your Fundamentals should be described and on display for customers, prospects, and potential recruits to see when they visit the site.

Screen-savers

Depending on your technology platform, you may be able to program everyone's screen saver so that it always shows the Fundamental of the Week. If you use a back-office system to run your operation, you may be able to program it so that when people log in each day, the first thing they see is the FOW.

"Way Cards"

Patterned after what I had seen Ritz-Carlton do, at RSI we created a wallet-size Z-fold card that all employees carried, listing each Fundamental and its description. Today, we have the same type of card for High Performing Culture and we create these for virtually every one of our clients. We call them "Way Cards" because we often call our Fundamentals the "HPC Way" or the "ABC Way" for any given company. These cards are great for all employees to carry, and they're equally valuable to give to clients, prospects, recruits, vendors, and other partners as a physical representation of your culture.

Flip Books

Flip books are another way to display the Fundamentals at people's work stations and in conference rooms. These are 5 x 7 "books" that fold into a table stand so that the FOW can be easily seen. We call them "flip books" because they're spiral bound in such a way that you can flip to the next FOW at the beginning of each week.

E-mail signatures

Your e-mail signature is another great place to display your FOW. At HPC, we each update our e-mail signatures at the beginning of every week so that it always shows the Fundamental, and many of our clients do the same. It's a subtle, but effective, reminder to us as well as to everyone with whom we communicate.

Other ideas

There are endless other ways to display your Fundamentals, and you're truly limited only by your own creativity. I've seen companies print them on t-shirts and employees can choose which Fundamental they want to wear each day. I've seen them printed on safety vests. I've seen them posted in the kitchen or even in the bathrooms (they'll certainly be seen there!). The more places we see them, the better.

Internal advertising

Think about the fact that companies spend literally billions upon billions of dollars each year on advertising. Have you ever taken a moment to consider why they do this? Quite simply, because it works! More specifically, the more we see messages, the more they tend to influence us. Whether we like it or not, the constant repetition of images or messaging makes them more likely to be top-of-mind, and as a result, they're more likely to affect our behavior.

The same is true here. The more we see our Fundamentals all around us, the more likely they're becoming our vocabulary, the more likely we're talking and thinking about them, and the more likely they're influencing our behavior.

As much as I've been talking about the power of "advertising" our Fundamentals, I want to be crystal clear here. In no way am I suggesting that we just have to put signs on our walls and we'll somehow change the culture, or that this is a replacement for everything else we need to do. Nothing could be further from the truth. This is *not* a replacement for the other steps in the 8-Step Framework. It's simply an easy and important element of *additional reinforcement* to everything else we're doing.

Other ways of communicating

So far, I've focused mostly on communicating about our culture through visual means. But of course, verbal communications are just as important. In Chapter 9, we'll talk more about weaving the language of the Fundamentals into your coaching sessions, and there are many other opportunities to communicate about them verbally as well.

In our exploration of rituals in Chapter 5, I talked about starting every meeting with a discussion of the FOW. At RSI, whenever we had company-wide meetings, in addition to the FOW, I would also do "acknowledgments." These were stories of exemplary performance by team members that I wanted to highlight for the rest of the staff. As I told each story, I would also highlight some of the different Fundamentals that the person exhibited. This is an easy way to keep reminding people of the Fundamentals and their applicability in day-to-day situations.

We have a number of clients who use reward and recognition programs to communicate about their Fundamentals. When an associate notices another person exhibiting the FOW, they write it up on a slip of paper and place it in a fish bowl. At the end of the week, the company holds a drawing and picks a winner to receive a gift card or other perk. Another simple, non-monetary approach is to require that any time a team member acknowledges another, she has to identify which Fundamental was being demonstrated. This keeps the Fundamentals at the forefront of everyone's mind.

> **The Fundamentals In Action**
>
> Pioneer Metal Finishing printed cards for each of their Pioneer Way Fundamentals. These cards are used by employees to acknowledge each other when they see a Fundamental in action. The front of the card shows the Fundamental, and the back of the card has space to describe the action that was observed. The completed card is given to the employee being acknowledged. At the end of each month, the cards are collected and a drawing is held to choose a winner for each Division. The winners are given an award, and are recognized in the company newsletter which is distributed by e-mail and posted on all central communication boards. Notes VP Shelly Gagen-Block, "We typically receive between 200 and 300 cards per month. Everyone is embracing our Fundamentals and they're really engaged in living the Pioneer Way."

The power of a common vocabulary

One of the biggest benefits of regular, consistent, and pervasive communication about your culture is that you develop a common vocabulary. For those who employ the Fundamentals System, the Fundamentals become your language. It just becomes the way people speak. You begin to hear conversations in which people remind each other to "practice blameless problem solving." Or they'll refer to the need to be a "generous listener" in this difficult situation. Or they'll push for greater precision in a conversation because they want to be "clear on expectations."

Here's an easy way to think of it: Imagine that each member of your team grew up in a different country, speaking a different language. When they come in to work, some speak Spanish but know just a little English. Others speak French but know a little Spanish. Still others speak German but know just a bit of French. As they try to work together, you can just picture the kind of struggles that are caused by their inability to fully understand each other.

> **The Fundamentals In Action**
>
> David Bennett is the CEO of Connections for Business, an IT managed services provider in South Florida. His 20 employees have been practicing their Fundamentals since early 2014. The power of this common vocabulary has been game-changing for him.
>
> "The biggest impact for us has been creating a common language. When we talk about these every week, and someone uses a phrase like 'Check the ego at the door' or 'Focus on solutions,' everyone immediately knows what that means and we adjust our behavior. It's given us a tool to communicate more effectively."

Now imagine that we created a new language that everyone learned together and agreed to speak when at work. Think of how much more smoothly and easily people could collaborate. How much more quickly problems could be solved. How much more effectively they could work together. The Fundamentals create that common language, and the more we communicate them, in all the different ways, the more ingrained they become.

In the next chapter, we'll see how this common language can be used to increase the effectiveness of our coaching, and in so doing, make our culture even more relevant on a day-to-day basis.

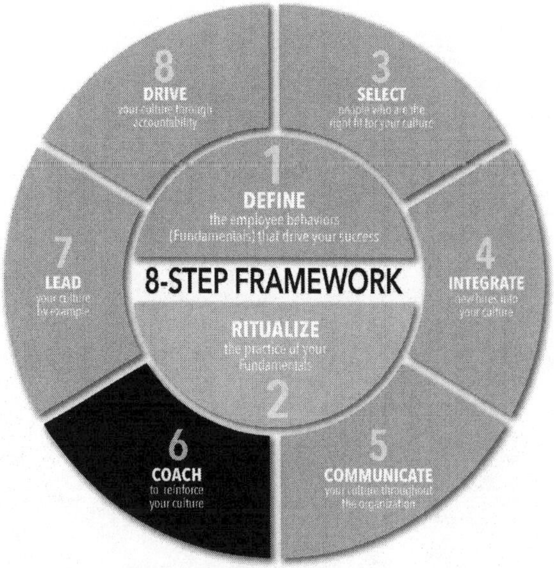

COACH to reinforce your culture

Throughout this book, I've emphasized the importance of seeing culture through a behavior lens, noting that your culture is best observed by looking not at the signs on your walls, but rather at the behavior of your people. We've talked about how to define your culture in terms of the behaviors (Fundamentals) you want to see, how to build rituals around teaching and practicing them, how to select and integrate people who exhibit those preferred behaviors, and even how to communicate about them. In this chapter, I want to turn our attention to exploring how we can further deepen the understanding and adoption of our Fundamentals through the use of coaching.

When I use the word "coaching" in this context, I'm referring to the way in which we provide people with feedback and guidance aimed at helping them improve their performance. Every day, your people are interacting with each other and the world, and any number of issues inevitably arise. Perhaps a customer calls with a thorny issue. Or two team members are struggling to get along. Or a project wasn't completed on time or to your satisfaction. As a manager or a leader, these situations provide you with incredibly valuable opportunities to apply the Fundamentals and help your people see their relevance. The most important way to do this is to be sure you use the specific language and vocabulary of your Fundamentals in your coaching session. Let me give you a couple of simple, but common, examples to illustrate what I mean.

Using the language of the Fundamentals

You take a call from a customer who's frustrated that one of your associates, Jerry, was supposed to get back to her with an answer last week and she still hasn't heard from him. When you check with Jerry, he explains that he didn't yet have the answer and so didn't see any point in calling the customer back with nothing substantive to report. In your coaching with Jerry, you might emphasize several Fundamentals. You might encourage Jerry to "walk in your customer's shoes" and help him to understand how the customer feels when she doesn't get a response. You might talk about being "a fanatic about response time" and how this includes keeping people updated on the status of their issues. You might emphasize the importance of "honoring commitments."

You could use a variety of ways to coach Jerry on how to handle the situation, but if you don't reference the Fundamentals in your coaching, you're missing a tremendous opportunity to connect the dots. By pointing out the applicable Fundamentals and using their specific language, you're helping to pull them off the wall and bring them into real life. You're making them relevant. Your associates begin to see that the Fundamentals aren't just signs on a wall or ideas you talk about in theoretical discussions. No, they're useful, practical guides for how we want to respond in real situations that happen every day.

Here's another example: A customer calls your service department, frustrated that a change was made to his service package and he wasn't notified. The service rep says it was the account manager's fault for not notifying the customer. The account manager says it was marketing's fault because they were supposed to be sending a communication to all customers. Marketing says it was product development's fault because they didn't provide marketing with enough lead-time to get the notice out. Sound familiar?

As you work with the various team members to provide coaching, you might emphasize the importance of "practicing blameless problem solving." You ask them to recall the three steps to blameless problem solving, and focus everyone on first taking care of the customer's immediate problem. Second, you have them diagnose the root cause of the issue, and third, you have them incorporate their learning into a process improvement that reduces the chance for this type of thing to happen in the future. Here again, if you approached the coaching without referring to and applying the relevant Fundamental(s), you would have missed a golden opportunity to further cement the team members' appreciation for how helpful the Fundamentals are as a guide for action.

Leveraging every situation to teach

There are two common, and naïve, misconceptions that I hear from leaders all the time. The first is the notion that if you set a good example, people will pick up on it and follow your lead, and as a result, you shouldn't have to teach these things. While I don't disagree with the importance of setting a good example (more on that in the next chapter), that's clearly not enough. People aren't going to be able to simply observe you and somehow figure out everything that's important. Further, they may not even see you or their leaders often enough, and some of the examples they do see may not be ones you want them to emulate. No, if we want people to behave in a certain way, we also need to teach them overtly, and we must never stop teaching.

The second misconception is the notion that we shouldn't have to teach these things because it "ought to be common sense." Whether it ought to be common sense or not is largely irrelevant, as is whether or not we should have to teach the

The Fundamentals In Action

MHS Lift is a second-generation family business, located in NJ, that's been around for nearly 50 years. They sell and service forklifts and material handling supplies, and they employ just over 165 people. They've been practicing their Fundamentals since 2014 and their CEO, Andy Levin, loves to share this story:

"I had a situation where two of my service coordinators were literally yelling and screaming at each other. Rather than trying to mediate, I sat them in a room, gave them our Fundamentals card, and told them I'd be back in five minutes and I wanted them to look at the Fundamentals, decide which ones applied to this situation, and figure out how they were going to resolve it. Sure enough, when I came back in five minutes, they were laughing and smiling and had worked out their issue. This would never have happened before."

behaviors we want. The bottom line is that if we want our people to consistently operate in a certain way, then we have to articulate what we want with clarity, and we have to teach it over and over again. As leaders and managers, we play a pivotal role in this effort.

Recognizing this, we need to see every situation as a teaching moment. This sometimes requires us to slow down. As problem solvers, it's our natural tendency to want to jump in and start taking action, to give direction and make things happen. This is when it's important for us to slow down just a bit and recognize the teaching opportunity that's been presented. What do we want our people to learn from this? What Fundamentals can we further cement in how we talk about this situation? What does our culture say about how this situation should be handled? While it may feel like we're slowing things down, in the long run, we're actually gaining speed because we're helping to grow the capabilities of our people to handle more situations on their own, and in a way that's consistent with our culture.

I remember when I first learned this in my own leadership career. In the earliest days of RSI, the company consisted almost exclusively of people in my family. Believe it or not, at one time or another, all four of my siblings were involved, four of our spouses, my father, three cousins, and my best friend! When we had 15–20 employees, two-thirds of them were family. Since we all grew up in the same family, we didn't have to talk much about how things should be done. We shared a common upbringing and value system.

When we began to hire lots of people who weren't in my family, I realized that I couldn't just assume they would look at the world the same way that I did. I was very particular about the way I wanted our company to do things, and I recognized early on that the only way I could ensure that would happen was if I was clear in what I wanted and I taught it consistently. And that's exactly what I did. When I developed the Fundamentals, it was really just an extension and a codification of what I was already teaching.

In my years leading RSI, and in my role as the leader of HPC, I see every situation as a chance to teach. Rarely do I ever simply give an instruction. Instead, I take the opportunity to teach how I want us to think about the situation. This is what coaching is all about.

Annual Fundamentals training

Beyond using the day-to-day situations that arise as a forum for coaching and teaching, you can also create learning opportunities as a part of regular training. At RSI, in addition to the weekly rituals I've described, all employees attended annual Fundamentals training. The training typically lasted 1–2 hours and would give people the chance to apply their understanding of the Fundamentals to real scenarios.

As part of the training, we would create a series of scenarios describing situations that employees might reasonably expect to encounter. People would work in teams and we would ask them to decide how they would handle the situation and which of our Fundamentals would most guide their behavior. The team participation would allow people to hear a variety of perspectives. In most cases, five or ten different Fundamentals would come into play. We'd typically give each team ten minutes to discuss the scenario and develop their answer, and then we'd have different teams share what they came up with, once again leveraging the power of the entire group for additional insights. This also gave me, as a leader, the chance to provide additional input and coaching, based on whatever I heard.

This kind of practice is important for several reasons. First, similar to the coaching examples I referred to earlier in this chapter, it helps people to see how practical and useful the Fundamentals are as a guide for dealing with everyday issues. Second, it reaffirms that our culture is not so much about discussing lofty concepts as it is about how we make day-to-day decisions in real situations. And third, it allows us sufficient opportunity to practice responding to situations in the "lab" so that we're more likely to respond appropriately when the scenario happens for real.

Coaching, the sixth step in the 8-Step Framework, is how you help people connect the theoretical with the practical. It's the guidance you provide to ensure that the "curriculum" of your culture is understood and practiced with consistency.

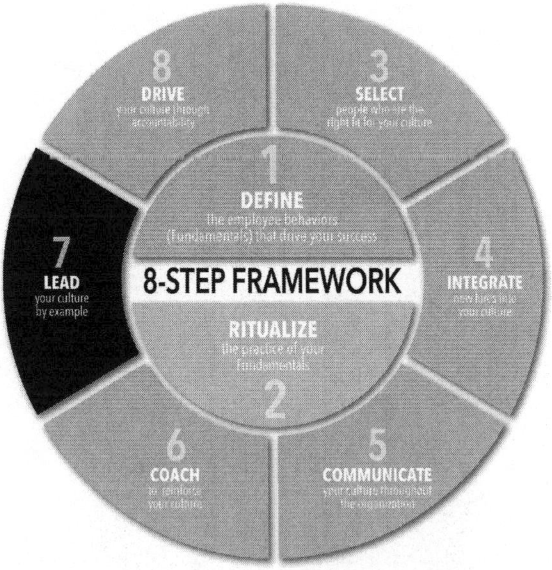

LEAD your culture by example

In the last chapter, I talked about the importance of demonstrating the relevance of your culture by leveraging day-to-day situations as opportunities to teach and coach, and specifically about working the language of the Fundamentals into your coaching. And while the verbal lessons we provide our people are tremendously impactful, there may be no greater lesson than the one we teach by our own example. It's why I call the seventh step in the 8-Step Framework, "Leading by example."

Whether it's fair or not, our people are observing us every minute of every day, consciously and unconsciously, and they're taking their cue from us about what really matters. We can talk all day long about delivering legendary service, but how we respond to a difficult customer issue will have more impact than anything we say. We can explain the three steps to blameless problem solving, but the way we react when the &^%#@ hits the fan will teach far more than our words do.

Not only are our people learning from everything that we do, they're even learning from everything we *don't* do! If we're sloppy about punctuality, they learn that honoring commitments isn't important. If we don't get back to people quickly, they learn that being a fanatic about response time isn't that critical. And if we see team members behaving in ways that run counter to what we profess our culture to be and we don't address it, we're teaching people that those behaviors are, in fact, acceptable.

Two implications

While the notion that your actions speak louder than your words is certainly not novel, there are two important implications that follow from a deep appreciation of this phenomenon. The first implication is that you become much more cognizant of setting the right example in everything you do. Before you act, you take a moment to reflect on what you want to demonstrate by what you're about to do. You raise the level of intentionality in your actions, fully aware of their impact on those around you.

The second implication of this increased awareness is that you begin to look at your own behavior in a much more critical or analytic way. Unless we're perfect, there are always areas in which we occasionally fall short of demonstrating the behaviors we want to teach. That's simply part of being human. Great leaders however, recognize these shortcomings and, more importantly, they intentionally work to improve upon them.

A personal example

Let me offer a personal example here to illustrate what I mean by working on our shortcomings. One of our core Fundamentals at RSI was to practice "meaningful acknowledgment and appreciation." To be clear, I'm not talking about giving everyone a trophy because they showed up for work. That's actually destructive on a variety of levels. Rather, I'm referring to true, honest, robust acknowledgment. I knew that when people felt genuinely appreciated, it made for a more enriching environment and it caused people to perform at a higher level. The problem, however, was that I wasn't very good at doing this.

You see, I grew up in a family with very high expectations. In my family, if you got straight As in school, it was pretty much par for the course. If my friends got straight As, they got taken out to dinner, but in my family, it was just expected. And to be truthful, that wasn't a problem for me. It's just the way I grew up.

When I first became a leader, I figured that if I hired really good people, they'd do great work, and they wouldn't need or expect to hear much from me. It didn't take long before I realized the problem: They didn't all grow up in my family! And it turns out that most people thrive in environments in which there's plenty of meaningful appreciation. Though I eventually learned how important this was, it didn't come very naturally to me and I struggled to set a good example.

So, here's what I did. I happen to be a pretty organized person, and I use an electronic task management tool to keep track of everything I need to accomplish in a day, a week, or a month. In the system that I use, there's a way of setting up repeating tasks—things I may want to do every Friday, or every 15th of the month, or every third Wednesday. Many years ago, I set up two repeating tasks that would come up every three days. The first one said, "Do a written acknowledgment." The second one said, "Do a personal acknowledgment." By having these constant reminders, I forced myself to pay more attention to the things around me that were worthy of acknowledgment and made sure that I acted upon them. Eventually, I turned this from one of my weaknesses as a leader into one of my strengths.

I share this story simply as a way of demonstrating a level of seriousness about paying attention to the example I'm setting and working on my shortcomings. Where are the areas of your culture in which you fall short of setting the best example, and what are you prepared to do about it? This is what I mean by being serious about your leadership example.

You don't have to be perfect

As a leader, you obviously don't have to be perfect and, in fact, never will be. However, you should at least be an excellent example of the culture you're trying to promote, or you'll be undermining your own efforts.

Interestingly, when you occasionally fall short, if handled properly and with humility, it can be an even greater example of leadership than if you didn't make mistakes. Let's suppose that in the heat of working through a challenging customer situation you came down hard on one of your staff without even knowing all the facts. The next day, you apologize to the person, letting her know that you had failed to practice blameless problem solving, and asking for her support as you work to improve. If done in a genuine way, you're showing your humanity and demonstrating that we all must work to improve. Of course, if you continue to repeat this behavior, you'll ultimately lose credibility and your apology will have no value.

While it's OK to make mistakes, there's a big difference between showing that you're human and are working on your shortcomings, and acting as if the Fundamentals don't apply to you. Repeated violations are likely to send the message that the culture is something everyone else should work on, but you're exempt. Given the importance of your example, nothing could be more damaging than that.

When I talk about leading by example in this chapter, I'm referring to all the various leaders in your organization. As they work with their teams, the example they set shows people the true culture of the organization. Yet, as influential as these leaders are, no one has the same influence as the CEO.

> **The Fundamentals In Action**
>
> As the CEO of Coastal Construction Products, a Jacksonville, FL-based distributor of specialty construction materials with nearly 200 employees, Martin Harrell understands how important his own example is in setting the culture for his company. And yet, he's not always perfect. "One time, I was working with a member of my executive team preparing for an important client presentation. We worked on our parts separately and then combined them. When I compared my work to his, I was honestly embarrassed. I realized I hadn't demonstrated our Fundamental, 'Make Quality Personal' at nearly the level he had; so I apologized and reworked my portion to make it something I was proud of. I often share this story with new members to our team because I want them to see that I'm not always perfect, but that I'm darn serious about our Fundamentals, and am working on myself to constantly get better."

The "Chief Cultural Officer"

I'm sometimes asked about the factors that most correlate with success in building a high-performing culture. Without question, the single biggest factor is what I call, "CEO sponsorship."

While the CEO doesn't have to *do* everything, she must be the biggest driver of the culture. She must be the one who's most passionate about it and works to ensure that it's one of the biggest corporate priorities. When the inevitable compromises arise, whether it's the temptation to hire someone who's not a good cultural fit, or you're considering skipping integration, or you're hesitant to let go of a toxic person because they produce a lot of business, someone must be the loud, clear advocate for your culture. And no one carries the same political or emotional clout as the CEO. That's why I describe the CEO as the "Chief Cultural Officer." The CEO quite literally owns the culture.

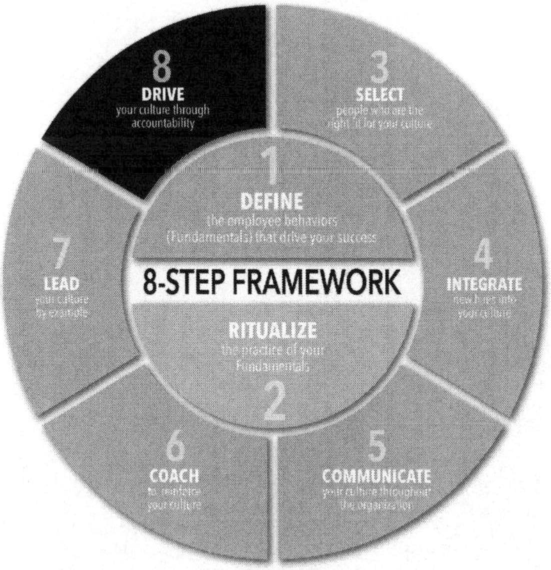

DRIVE your culture through accountability

In the previous chapter, I talked about the importance of leading by example and the recognition that our actions ultimately speak louder than our words. The last step in our 8-Step Framework, driving the culture through accountability, is the logical extension of this thought. It's how we show our people, ourselves, and the world that we're not kidding, that we're actually serious about our culture. Without accountability, our efforts amount to little more than wishful thinking.

Surveys

One way to hold ourselves accountable is through surveying. This is a tool we used extensively at RSI, and we do with most of our clients as well. While we conducted a variety of different surveys about our performance, our primary cultural survey was specifically oriented toward our Fundamentals. For each Fundamental, we wrote a statement of what it would look like if we were doing this behavior well. For example, for the Fundamental called "Honor commitments," the statement might read, "Our employees do what they say they're going to do, when they say they're going to do it." That's what we mean by honoring commitments.

We designed the survey to evaluate how consistently we exhibited each behavior, using the following descriptors:

- Almost always
- Usually
- Sometimes
- Seldom
- Never

Then we'd convert this to a numeric scale with "Almost always" being a 5 and "Never" being a 1. In this way, we could calculate an overall score for how well we were living to our Fundamentals, from an external perspective, and we could measure our progress from year to year. We could also put a number on each individual Fundamental, and work on our lower scoring ones to improve our performance.

Each year, the survey was sent to three different groups: our customers, our vendors and suppliers, and our own employees. It was essentially the same survey, but we wanted to tabulate the results separately by group. We also provided space for respondents to give any open-ended feedback they wanted to offer. In our current version of the survey, we've added a Net Promoter Score (NPS) question which has people state how likely they'd be to recommend us, on a 1–10 scale, to their friends and relatives.

While the survey, of course, isn't perfect, it does give us some data on how well we're living to our culture and it allows us to measure improvement over time. As importantly, it sends a clear message to our own team as well as the outside world that we're pretty darn serious. Serious enough to be transparent and to hold ourselves accountable for what we say is important to us.

Performance reviews

Another great way to drive accountability is through the performance review system. Interestingly, when I ask workshop participants if their performance review process includes any elements of their culture, typically fewer than 25% of people answer positively. If I were an employee in your company, and I were sitting down with my manager to go through a performance review, whatever that looks like for you, and nowhere in the conversation was there any discussion of our culture, what conclusion would I likely come to? Probably that it's not very important. It's obviously not the only thing we'd be talking about, but it surely ought to be in there somewhere. And of course, it would be difficult to include it in performance reviews if we didn't have much clarity about what our culture was in the first place!

With 25–30 Fundamentals, it's not practical to include them all in your performance reviews. Instead, I recommend choosing the 4–6 Fundamentals that are most relevant for each position. While we, of course, want all employees to practice all the Fundamentals, there may be certain ones that are especially relevant for a salesperson and different ones for a bookkeeper. Having selected the appropriate Fundamentals, you can then use the same evaluation method I described for the survey. You might even have the employee and the manager each do the evaluation and then use the result as the basis for discussion.

Incidentally, I much prefer the descriptive phrases like "almost always," "usually," etc. over a purely numerical scale because people have such varying ideas about what the number means. One person's "4" is another person's "3." And some people never give a "5," just on principle. I also prefer "almost always" rather than "always" because it avoids the trap of the person who says, "Well, no one is perfect. They don't *always* do this." The phrase "almost always" seems to better capture the spirit of what we mean.

The ultimate accountability

While there are many different ways to demonstrate accountability for your culture, one stands out as the most significant indication of your seriousness: terminating a relationship that adds value to the organization, but comes at too high a cost in terms of its impact on your culture. Most frequently, the relationship is with a key employee; but sometimes, it can actually be with a customer. Let's look at each separately.

Virtually every company I see has at least one person who they've been struggling with seemingly forever. This person wreaks havoc in the organization; he's opposite of everything we say is important to us and we talk about him in every management meeting, but he's still here. Anecdotally, roughly 80% of these people tend to be salespeople, 10% are usually in finance, and 10% usually have some type of technical skill. And what do they all have in common that makes us hesitant to let them go? They provide something that we're afraid of losing. If it's the typical salesperson, as disruptive as she is, she also produces a tremendous amount of business or manages some of our most important customer relationships. If it's the finance person, she's been here so long that we're afraid of losing all that institutional knowledge. If it's the guy with a technical skill, he has a level of expertise that's very difficult to find in the marketplace, and we shudder to think of where we'd be without him or how we'd find someone to replace him. Sound familiar? I'll bet.

> **The Fundamentals In Action**
>
> "If there's one thing I've learned, it's that there has to be buy-in from top to bottom," admits Jerry Schill, CEO of Schill Grounds Management, a Cleveland-based firm with more than 100 team members. "I learned this lesson the hard way with one of the brightest and most productive people I ever hired," he adds. Though this person added great value, he was a constant source of internal friction and was decidedly out-of-step with the SGM Way.
>
> After exhausting every means of support he could provide, Jerry was left with no choice. "I finally had to look at myself in the mirror and realize that I couldn't talk about our Fundamentals every single day and then keep turning a blind eye to this person's behavior. He was ultimately released and the entire organization knew for sure just how serious we were about our culture."

We've essentially allowed ourselves to be held hostage by these people because we're afraid to lose them. And all the while, we're sending a loud clear message to our entire organization. We're telling everyone, "Our culture is very important here, *unless you produce enough business*!" I often tell my workshop participants that the best way for me to really know your culture is to "look at the behavior that you tolerate." Regardless of the statements on your website or what you tell people on the first day, what you're willing to tolerate is the true measure of your culture. And by the way, while we're worrying about the potential impact of losing the contributions of one of these people, we often fail to recognize that we're also making some of our very best team members vulnerable. Eventually, our best people are going to get fed up watching this behavior be tolerated, and they may decide to go elsewhere.

Nearly all leaders have, at some point in their career, had to fire one of these difficult people. Interestingly, when I ask them about this experience and how others reacted, I always hear the same thing: "They all said 'it's about time' or 'thank you'." And when I ask those same leaders what they said to themselves afterward, they'll all say, practically in unison, "What took me so long?" or "I should've done that a long time ago!" What's even more fascinating is that almost never do they lose the things they feared losing that had kept them from making the decision. The team typically bands together and picks up any slack so that the organization can move forward more successfully and smoothly than ever before.

The Fundamentals In Action

Dan Berger, CEO of Berger Rental Communities, leaves no room for doubt when it comes to his commitment to the Berger Way. If a tenant is continuously abusive to his staff, Berger will refuse to renew their lease. More notably, last year they fired one of their largest customers. This property owner, for whom Berger managed property, represented nearly 20% of Berger's annual revenues! But despite repeated discussion, the customer refused to conduct business in a way that was consistent with Berger's culture. For Dan, the choice was clear. "I needed to show my employees just how serious I was about my support for them and our culture, so the decision was easy, though it was certainly painful," notes Dan.

Getting rid of these toxic team members sends a loud, clear message to your organization about how serious you are when it comes to culture. Those sitting on the fence about the culture start to understand, in no uncertain terms, that it's time to get on board or leave.

Interestingly, terminating a customer relationship can send an even louder message. Have you ever had a customer who was consistently abusive to your staff? Think of that customer with whom no one wants to work. The one who sees the world from a "win-lose" perspective. The one who clearly operates from an entirely different set of behavioral standards than that which you're trying to teach. When you continue to do business with these customers, you're telling your team that the revenue generated by the customer is more important than your culture. And conversely, when you terminate a high-revenue relationship, you send a particularly bold message to your organization about just how strongly you value your people and your culture. That's not easy to do, which is why the message is so powerful.

I recognize that this last section may sound a bit heavy-handed, and so I want to be clear that I'm a big advocate for coaching and mentoring, and working at relationships. I'm not suggesting that at the earliest sign of a problem we're simply dismissing team members or firing clients. In fact, quite the opposite is true. We should be doing everything we can to help our people to succeed within our environment, and we should be working to build cooperative, mutually beneficial customer relationships. But at some point, when we've been coaching long enough and not seeing the changes we want, the person or the customer no longer gets to continue working with us. That's what I'm referring to here. There truly is no greater way to demonstrate accountability for your culture than that.

This brings us to the end of our discussion of the 8-Step Framework. At this point, you've created your Fundamentals, you've determined what rituals would work best for your workforce, and you've got a good understanding of each of the elements of the framework. The piece I haven't yet explained though, is how to launch this within your organization. I call it the "Rollout," and that's our focus for Chapter 12.

The Rollout

When I was describing, in Chapter 4, who should be involved in the development of the Fundamentals, you may have been surprised that I was advocating for this to be a leadership function rather than a collaboration among all employees. "After all, this will never work if we don't engage the hearts and minds of our entire workforce," is the familiar refrain. And while I definitely agree with this premise, I noted earlier that we can more effectively accomplish that engagement by how we roll the program out, rather than by having everyone's input or participation from the beginning. And that's where we want to turn our attention next. How do we roll this out?

I often describe the rollout process as "setting the table for success." We could write the greatest set of Fundamentals, and we could develop brilliant rituals, but if we don't achieve that all-important level of engagement among our people, we're seriously jeopardizing our chances for success. The rollout is where we give context and meaning for this effort, where we explain what we're doing and why, and where we generate the enthusiasm and participation that will be necessary if we're to have a meaningful and lasting impact. It's that important.

There are three principles that we must keep in mind as we plan the rollout:

1. It should include as close to 100% of the workforce as is possible.
2. It should be as minimally disruptive to the business operation as possible, while accepting the fact that it will, in fact, be at least somewhat disruptive.
3. It should provide for as much participation on the part of all team members as possible.

With those principles in mind, let me describe the most effective way to conduct the rollout process, based on trial and error and the experience of doing this with more than 200 different organizations.

Preparation

Like most events, the better prepared you are, the more smoothly the event goes off. Accordingly, there are a few things you need to attend to in advance:

- **Session size.** We've found the ideal session size to be between 25 and 35 people, with a maximum of roughly 50. While it can be done successfully with larger groups, it's far more difficult to make sure that everyone participates when the group is more than 50 people.
- **Scheduling.** The ideal rollout is three hours long, and it starts and finishes on time. This means you'll need to figure out how to organize your people, and where appropriate, coverage for them, so that everyone can attend one session.
- **Advance notice.** I think it's important to briefly introduce the Fundamentals to team members prior to their actual rollout meeting. We usually

print a wallet-sized Z-fold card that lists the Fundamentals and their descriptions and suggest that a card be mailed to each person at her home address, timed to arrive approximately 2–4 days before the meeting. The card should be accompanied by a letter from the CEO briefly explaining what it is. The timing is effective in generating some "buzz" prior to the rollout, without the necessity of going into a full and detailed explanation.

- **Small teams.** Within each session, people should be subdivided into groups of 3–4 people (3 is ideal, and 4 is acceptable), for purposes of small group discussion. If possible, it's best to group people who don't usually work together or are in different functions, as this facilitates an even better exchange of perspectives. Three-person groups work well because everyone has an opportunity to contribute and it's more difficult for one person to "hide" and avoid participating.
- **Room setup.** The room should be set up in such a way that the members of each group are sitting together. It's helpful to have tent cards or something similar (like at a wedding) to indicate the seating location for each group. Each team member should have a nametag with their name printed in large letters and their group number in small print. If your office, shop, or plant doesn't have a room that's of sufficient size to accommodate the rollout, you may want to consider using an offsite location such as a hotel or meeting hall.

- **Developing scenarios.** In one of the exercises, teams are going to be discussing the Fundamentals and how they apply in situations that typically happen in your organization. It's best if the leadership team can develop a handful of good scenarios, in advance, to be used in this exercise.

Conducting the rollout

- **Length.** While three hours no doubt sounds challenging, or even intimidating, my experience is that it's entirely appropriate and necessary, and so it's worth finding a way to make it happen. Surprisingly, most team members will comment on how fast the time went and how much they enjoyed the session.
- **Structure.** The three-hour session typically breaks down as follows:
    - Introduction (10–15 mins)
    - Exercise 1 (90–105 mins)
    - Break (10 mins)
    - Exercise 2 (40–50 mins)
    - Wrap-up (10 mins)

The Fundamentals In Action

Batory Foods is an $800-million distributor of food ingredients, headquartered in Chicago, IL. Founded in 1979, they've grown to include 470 team members working in locations across the US. Not surprisingly, the process of rolling out their Fundamentals (they call them the "Batory Basics") was complex, given the size and distribution of their workforce. Despite the logistical challenges, their CEO, Ron Friedman, attended every one of the rollout sessions in every location!

Says Ron, "If I was going to ask my team for their commitment, I needed to first show them my own level of personal commitment. That isn't something that can be delegated. I wanted them to see that this wasn't going to be the 'flavor of the month' but instead, was something that would become part of our DNA."

- **CEO participation.** Ideally, the CEO should attend every session and introduce why the culture is so important to the organization's success. CEO participation is a demonstration of organizational commitment from the top. If this just isn't practical, then the highest-ranking executive at the location should play this role.
- **Introduction.** During the opening, the facilitator explains the importance of culture, introduces the idea of the Fundamentals, describes the rituals that will be practiced moving forward, and explains the logistics for the day.
- **Exercise 1.** The purpose of the first exercise is to give each team a chance to explore every Fundamental and think about what it means to them. The facilitator breaks the Fundamentals into

groups of 5–6 at a time. He takes the first 5 (or 6) and briefly explains the essence of each. Then he asks each team to discuss the first 5 Fundamentals amongst themselves, sharing with each other, from their personal perspectives, which one of the first group they like the most and why, and which one they find to be the most challenging to practice and why. The facilitator allows roughly five minutes for the teams to discuss and then asks for volunteers to share their thoughts with the larger group. Each person's comments can be leveraged or expanded upon for further teaching. This process is then repeated for Fundamentals 6–10, 11–15, and so on until all Fundamentals have been discussed.

- **Break.** It's helpful to have light snacks and drinks available during the break, ideally close to the meeting room so that people can be back in their seats within 10–15 minutes.
- **Exercise 2.** The purpose of the second exercise is to give people a chance to see how the Fundamentals serve as useful and practical guides for behavior that are relevant in everyday situations they face. The facilitator describes one of the scenarios that was previously developed (see note under **Preparation**) and asks each team to discuss how they would handle such a situation and which Fundamentals would most guide their behavior. Teams are given five minutes to discuss and then the facilitator asks several teams to share their findings. As with the first exercise, team comments can be leveraged for further teaching.

- **Wrap-up.** In the wrap-up, the facilitator reminds people of the importance of practice and the various ways they'll be practicing the Fundamentals through the use of rituals. It's also helpful to remind people to coach and support each other as they work to develop new habits.

Alternative approaches

The program I've delineated on the previous pages is obviously far easier when all of your team members are in one location, when they all speak English, and when they all work in an office. Of course, those conditions don't describe reality for many organizations, so let me offer some helpful suggestions for dealing with a variety of alternative challenges:

- **Remote locations or workers.** There is a variety of ways to handle remote locations or workers. Generally, if the location has 15 or more people, I think it's best to go to that location and deliver the rollout in person. With smaller groups, it may not be practical or cost-effective to do so. In cases like these, video conferencing can work surprisingly well. With advances in technology, people working in remote locations can participate almost as if they were in the room with the rest of the teams. Another approach is to use an eLearning tool to have remote people learn about the culture and the Fundamentals at a time that's more convenient to them. While this approach loses the impact of group discussion, it does provide considerably more flexibility.

- **Shift work.** If associates work round-the-clock shifts, rollout sessions can be scheduled in such a way that you catch people at the beginning or end of a shift. Given people's fatigue at the end, earlier is typically better if it can be done. My team has done rollout meetings at 11pm and 3am, among other times! If your company is small and can't close for three hours, you might consider closing an hour early and doing a session from 4–7 pm with pizza afterwards.
- **Language barriers.** Many construction and manufacturing companies, as well as those situated in the southeast and southwest, have significant portions of their workforce for whom English is not their primary language. In this case, it's best to print the Fundamentals in multiple languages, and to conduct separate rollout sessions in the most appropriate language. If you have bilingual leaders who can facilitate, this is ideal. Alternatively, you can bring in a bilingual facilitator.

The rollout process I've described, done effectively, creates a powerful and memorable experience for team members. The level of participation, engagement, and enthusiasm often surprises the leadership team, and they typically see people sharing with each other in ways that have rarely happened before.

I occasionally hear leaders balk at the thought of taking people out of work for three hours, given the financial and productivity cost of doing so; and I absolutely understand and appreciate the challenge it presents. At the same time, I don't think it's possible for me to overstate the importance of conducting the rollout effectively. While it no doubt requires a significant level of organizational commitment, it's simply not a place to compromise. If we fail to gain the full engagement of our people, we'll have seriously undermined the effectiveness of the effort. When you truly understand the impact your culture has on your success, you'll see that the investment you make up-front in rolling it out properly will pay significant dividends down the road.

The Fundamentals In Action

It would be hard to have more passion for culture than Marc Blaushild, CEO of Famous Enterprises in Akron, OH. Famous is a multi-generational family business that includes both distribution and manufacturing. With approximately 700 associates working in 37 locations primarily throughout the Midwest, rolling out their Fundamentals was no small task.

In the fall of 2015, Famous brought all their associates into the headquarters for the rollout, running 3-hour sessions every morning and afternoon for several weeks, and Marc attended every one! "Allowing people the time to go through the exercises and talk about all our Fundamentals was probably the most important part of everything we did," remembers Marc. "Shortening or compromising on the rollout would have undermined the program and what we stand for. How committed would we be to our culture if we weren't willing to spend the time or money giving every associate the opportunity to fully embrace our Fundamentals?" he adds.

The Fundamentals System™

As you've no doubt clearly seen, the premise of this entire book is the recognition that culture plays an enormous role in organizational performance and that, as leaders, we should be both intentional and systematic in designing the culture we want, rather than living with the culture that happens by chance. The 8-Step Framework provides the roadmap for the steps it takes to accomplish this goal.

While the 8-Step Framework provides the roadmap, I've also alluded throughout this book to the Fundamentals System™. The Fundamentals System refers to the specific set of products and tools we've developed over time to help organizations more successfully implement the Framework. In this chapter, I'll give you a brief overview of the elements that currently comprise that system. You can always learn more about these tools and see the latest version of the system by going to High Performing Culture's website: **(www.highperformingculture.com).**

Way Cards

It's helpful to have some kind of printed, physical representation of your culture that employees can keep with them and that can be shared with others. We've found that wallet-size or pocket-size Z-fold cards accomplish this task nicely. We call them "Way Cards" because they describe the "way" your company operates.

Flip Books

Flip books are an excellent way to keep the Fundamental of the Week visible. These 5 x 7 booklets with a folding stand sit at desktops, in conference rooms, in cubicles, and at the reception desk. Each week, the page is "flipped" so that the appropriate Fundamental is always on display.

eMinder™

eMinder is the automated software tool I described in Chapter 5 that sends a weekly lesson to each employee and then provides appropriate feedback. This tool helps to keep all team members engaged in the Fundamental of the Week and also provides important measurement and accountability. Management can run reports by person, department, or location to analyze data in a variety of ways.

CultureWise™

CultureWise is an eLearning tool primarily used during integration to introduce new employees to your culture. This 2–3 hour course explains why culture is so important, describes the rituals your company practices, and then teaches associates about each of your Fundamentals. The course includes graphics, animated videos, and questions and answers to test and ensure the comprehension of each Fundamental.

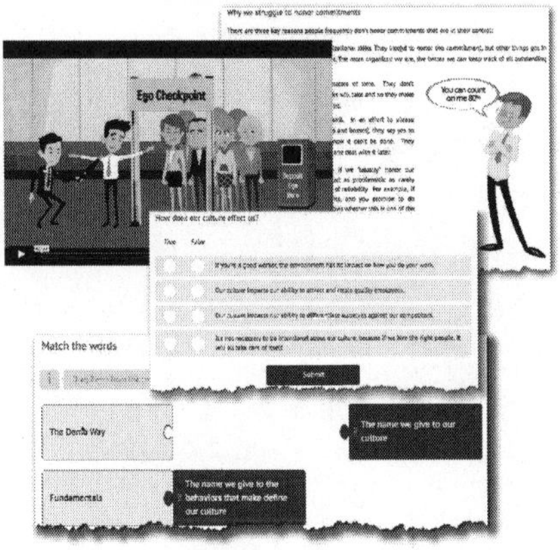

Coaching Guides

Written for managers and supervisors, and customized for each company's Fundamentals, the Coaching Guide is a valuable resource to help leaders use the Fundamentals in their daily work with staff. The guide is filled with teaching points, coaching tips, and great questions for discussion on each one of a company's Fundamentals.

Fundamentals Leadership Workshop and eCoach™

This highly interactive full-day workshop for managers and supervisors combines teaching along with role-plays and exercises to help them hone their skills as effective coaches of the Fundamentals. The eCoach module significantly increases participants' retention of their learning by sending 21 weekly follow-up lessons based on the content covered in the workshop.

Integration Training

Integration Training is a robust program designed to assist organizations in building world-class processes for bringing on new team members. The program includes a full assessment of a company's current program, a set of ready-to-implement recommendations, and access to a series of forms, templates, and documents collectively known as the HPC Integration Toolkit.

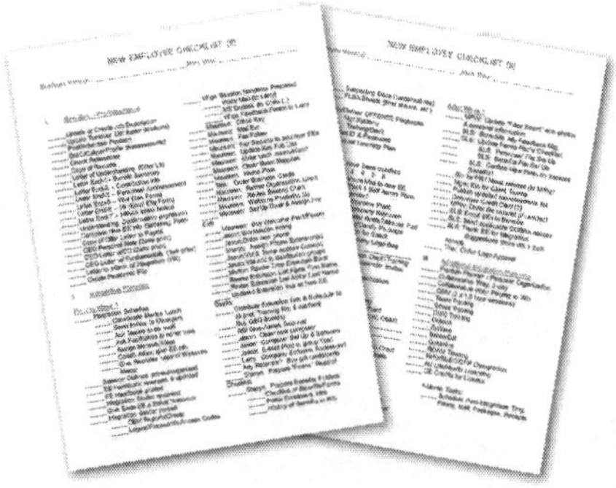

Culture Communications

In Chapter 8, I discussed the importance of communicating your culture in a pervasive way throughout your organization. This tool includes a suite of digital and graphic design services to help a company create and deploy a variety of visual communication tools throughout the workplace.

Fundamentals Surveys

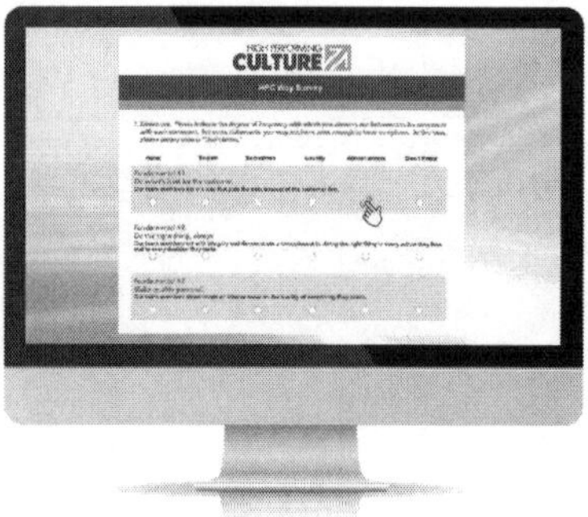

In Chapter 11, I talked about the importance of creating accountability for your culture and I described the survey we recommend to measure how consistently you're practicing your Fundamentals as well as how you improve over time. High Performing Culture (HPC) can write, deploy, and report on this survey, and also provide benchmark data comparing you to the rest of HPC's client base.

Fundamentals Video Tutorial Series

Available as part of the Fundamentals subscription service called HPCAccess™, the tutorial series includes dozens of four- to eight-minute videos with deeper teaching about specific Fundamentals. The series also includes discussion guides for each Fundamental that can be used as the foundation for more in-depth exploration of the Fundamental and its many facets.

HPCAccess™

HPCAccess is a subscription-based program that gives companies a variety of value-added benefits from unlimited access to senior consultants to use of the video tutorial series to participation in the online community HPC Exchange.

Annual Culture Summit

Each year, leaders who are passionate about building powerful, high-performing cultures gather for several days of learning and networking, and for sharing best practices. This event, facilitated and led by HPC senior staff, is usually held in the fall, and attracts CEOs and other senior leaders from around the country.

Lessons Learned

Having worked with so many different organizations, helping them to more intentionally create their cultures, I've been asked every conceivable question. While I've covered most of them throughout the body of this book, I want to use this chapter to share thirteen questions, and of course, their answers, that haven't been addressed elsewhere. In no particular order, let me share them with you here in an attempt to give you as complete an understanding as possible.

Q: How do you measure the return on investment in this work?

A: This is one of the most common questions I hear. While I read articles that quote impressive statistics about higher profits or lower turnover or increased productivity, I don't like to make those claims, mostly because we can't isolate the variables. In other words, if you increased sales by 50% this year, was that because you introduced a new product, you hired three new salespeople, your largest competitor went out of business, or because you worked on your culture? It's likely a combination of all of them.

There are some things that we *can* measure, though. We can measure the degree of engagement in our culture by analyzing participation rates in the eMinder software I referred to in Chapters 5 and 13. We can measure how well we're living to our culture through the annual survey that I described in Chapters 11 and 13. And it's certainly not a big leap of faith to suggest that if we're more consistently doing the behaviors that create success, it has to be a significant contributor to our improved results.

> **The Fundamentals In Action**
>
> "I can't say that the Fundamentals were 100% responsible, but I don't believe it's a coincidence that in the three years since we implemented them, our sales have doubled and our profits have quadrupled. I just can't believe that it didn't play a huge role." – Andy Levin, CEO of MHS Lift Co.

Q: How long does it take to see a difference?

A: The answer to this question, or course, depends on a variety of factors. Like losing weight, the more you have to lose, the more quickly you're likely to notice changes. Having said that, we typically see a difference even in the first few weeks. In particular, team members almost always begin using the language of the Fundamentals right away, and the impact of employing this common language is significant. Secondly, almost right away we see associates responding to daily issues and challenges differently, and more effectively, because they're applying the Fundamentals. Again, this typically happens within the first weeks of rolling out Fundamentals. The impact only grows from there.

Q: Shouldn't we do an assessment of our current culture before we begin our work on defining our Fundamentals?

A: This is one of those places where I'm going to buck conventional wisdom, but when I explain why, I think you'll see my point. Traditional thinking would suggest that before we can know where we're going, we first have to clearly understand where we are today. While this may be true, and even critical, when looking for directions in Google Maps, the same logic doesn't hold when trying to build the culture we want.

Remember that in the 8-Step Framework, we begin by defining, with tremendous clarity, what we want our culture to be. In Chapter 4, I called this a "design function." We're designing the extraordinary company we're trying to create, much as an architect might design a house. Regardless of the current state of our culture, we still need to define what we want to build for the future. If I did an assessment, and better understood how our people saw our current culture, how would it change my design? Not at all. I would still need to determine the Fundamentals that are most important to me, and I'd still need to practice them in the same way. It might take longer for us to achieve great success depending on our starting point, but it wouldn't change the steps I need to take nor the process for taking them.

As I discussed in Chapter 11, I *am* in favor of doing a survey or assessment after we roll out the Fundamentals, but the purpose of this survey is to get a baseline from which to measure our improvement, rather than to get more data to inform the design process. If the design process is the same regardless of the results of the initial assessment, I see no material value in doing the assessment.

Q: My CEO won't go for this. What should I do?

A: As I noted in Chapter 10, the single most important ingredient in the success of a culture initiative is what I call "CEO sponsorship." By sponsorship, I don't mean that the CEO has to do everything; rather that she's the one with the most passion and commitment for the culture, and that passion fuels the initiative. The reason this is so important is that the CEO is typically the only one with sufficient political weight to ensure that working on the culture remains a priority when other initiatives inevitably compete for attention. She's also the one with the authority to make sure we don't let short-term expediency override our commitment to only hiring the right people and making sure everyone goes through a proper integration.

Given my comments about the importance of CEO sponsorship, if you're in an organization where the CEO isn't yet on board, it would be best to exhaust all possibilities to get her alignment before going to Plan B. If you've tried everything you can to get the CEO on board, and it just isn't going to happen, then Plan B is to at least intentionally create the culture of the team you lead (assuming you're a leader). You can go through pretty much the same process with a sales team or an engineering department or whatever other team you may lead. While I don't say this in a flippant way, if you have no leadership role, and you're in an organization that isn't committed to building a first rate culture, you might consider whether or not that's a good place for you to stay.

Q: We have too many competing priorities to work on this now. When is the best time?

A: Much like the old saying about the best time to plant a tree, the best time to work on your culture was last year. The second best time is right now. More to the point, as we talked about in Chapter 1, your culture is the primary driver of employee performance and is a key factor in creating a sustainable competitive advantage. It's hard to imagine a more important initiative. Further, your culture is the foundation on which all your other strategic initiatives are built. Get the culture right, and all the other initiatives are likely to be more successful. Neglect or delay working on your culture, and you put the success of those other initiatives at risk.

Q: What if we don't have many meetings?

A: As I noted in Chapter 5, starting every meeting with the Fundamental of the Week is a particularly effective ritual because it helps to shift our teaching from being only episodic to becoming more systematic. Of course, if you don't have many meetings, this is less relevant.

The first thing I'd say is that I'm *not* an advocate of creating a meeting just to talk about the Fundamental if there's no other relevant business purpose for the meeting. However, if you don't currently have some type of daily "huddle" in most departments, you might consider creating one as an effective way of making sure all team members are on the same page and ready to work. This would then be a good forum in which to engage people with the Fundamental. Again, I wouldn't suggest this if it doesn't otherwise make good business sense in your environment.

In the rare times that you do have a meeting, it's important to leverage that opportunity to discuss the Fundamental. You might also consider scheduling some occasional "lunch and learn" sessions. These could be optional, but would create an opportunity for more extensive exploration of one or more Fundamentals. And of course, in the absence of meetings, you still may have opportunities to use e-mail to communicate thoughts about the Fundamental. You could even set up a "chat room" or other mechanism for people to engage with each other about the week's Fundamental.

Q: What if most of my employees don't have e-mail?

A: In many production or distribution environments, employees don't always have a company e-mail address. There are several methods I've seen companies use in these situations. You might first consider collecting personal e-mail addresses. Nearly everyone now has a smart phone and a personal e-mail address, and you may want this information for your personnel records anyway.

> **The Fundamentals In Action**
>
> "Though many of our warehouse and driver associates don't use our company e-mail addresses, we still want them to participate in eMinder each week. So we utilize their personal e-mails for all these team members, and our overall company participation in eMinder is consistently between 85% and 95% each week."
> —Marc Blaushild, CEO of Famous Enterprises

In some of our manufacturing clients, the plant manager prints the Fundamental of the Week e-mail and discusses it with workers in a huddle meeting. In others, they post the e-mail wherever other notices are displayed. Some companies even print the e-mail and include it in payroll envelopes. We have at least one company that posts the Fundamental of the Week and the relevant thoughts on Facebook each week.

Q: Does this work if we have a partnership group (CPA firm, law firm, e.g.)?

A: Yes. We've successfully implemented the Fundamentals in all kinds of organizations, including professional partnerships like law firms, CPA firms, engineering firms, and medical practices. At the same time, these types of organizations do have some unique elements that create different challenges. First is that they usually have a managing partner who doesn't have the same authority over the group's direction that a typical CEO would have. This just means that the process has to include a greater degree of consensus-building than might normally be suggested or necessary.

The second challenge can often be a more daunting one. Many of these organizations have a senior partner who's a particularly poor example of the desired culture, and the other partners lack the authority, or sometimes the will, to address the issue. Remember in Chapter 10 when we discussed the importance of the leadership example. It can be difficult to promote a culture if key leaders are setting a different example. This is an issue that's best addressed early on.

Q: We're making an acquisition. How do we integrate the new company into our culture?

A: As most know, the single biggest cause of failed mergers is a clash of cultures. Two companies may look great together on paper, but if their cultures can't be integrated, the merger is likely doomed. If you're the acquirer, the more institutionalized your culture is, the more easily you'll be able to integrate the new company into it. You can do a similar rollout for the new folks as you did for your own team, and then simply have everyone practicing the same weekly rituals.

If you're just about to go through a merger with a company of similar size, and haven't yet implemented the Fundamentals System, it may make sense to include the other company's leadership team in the development of the Fundamentals. This can help to create the new merged culture with both organizations feeling like important stakeholders.

Q: What's the best cycle for going through our Fundamentals—daily, weekly, or monthly?

A: My experience is that daily or weekly cycles work well, but less frequent than weekly significantly diminishes your effectiveness. As you may recall, I learned these concepts from Ritz-Carlton, and they cycle through their Basics one per day through the Daily Line-up. If your work schedule already includes daily huddles or "toolbox talks," the daily routine may work best. The advantage of a daily cycle is that each Fundamental is repeated more frequently. At the same time, this can be a disadvantage because you may struggle to find appropriate content to discuss with that much frequency.

With only a few exceptions, our clients cycle through their Fundamentals one per week. The weekly schedule still gives us a short enough time span to have an intensity of focus, while at the same time reducing the overall frequency of repetition. We can do a variety of different rituals all throughout the week so that there are multiple opportunities for engagement. While we may only go through a full cycle roughly twice per year (given the typical 25–30 Fundamentals), it should be noted that all of the Fundamentals are being talked about throughout the year as relevant situations arise. It's just that we have an increased focus on one particular Fundamental in any given week.

In my experience, going through a Fundamental every two weeks or every month just doesn't provide enough intensity of focus to have maximum impact. It's difficult to be thinking about a Fundamental all month long. Instead, we tend to think about it for a day, and then forget about it for the next 29 days until it's time for a new Fundamental.

Q: How do we keep it fresh?

A: This is one of the most frequently asked questions for companies that have been practicing their Fundamentals for a period of time. As I noted in Chapter 5, the most important element in keeping it fresh is to create more engagement. Ask questions in a meeting to get people participating rather than simply reciting the Fundamental. Rotate who's leading the discussion so that you get other perspectives. Rotate who's sending out the weekly message. The more people you involve and the more ways they participate, the fresher it will be.

While I've seen companies get very creative with games and contests around their Fundamentals, it's important to emphasize that the routine is the most important ingredient, as that's what helps us to sustain the necessary repetition. People don't constantly look for creative ways to change up the national anthem or how they brush their teeth. There's tremendous value in the constancy that comes from strong rituals or routines.

Q: How does this impact team members on a personal level?

A: Profoundly. It's pretty hard to practice Fundamentals at work and not have it impact your personal life as well. Learning to listen more generously or honor commitments or practice blameless problem solving or get clear on expectations is just as important at home as it is at work. Many people who worked with me at RSI continue to carry their Fundamentals card with them to this day, and they often tell me how practicing Fundamentals has changed them and enhanced their relationships. And we hear the same stories from clients all the time.

Q: Do these same concepts work outside of the business environment?

A: Absolutely. If you want to get any group of people to behave in a consistent manner, whether that group happens to be your employees, or it happens to be the athletes on your team or the students in your classroom or the children in your family, the same principles hold true. You dramatically improve your chances of success (there's never a guarantee) when you clearly articulate the behaviors you want to see and then you create a structured, systematic way to teach them over and over again.

I've actually helped several leaders to create Fundamentals for their family. In Appendix F, I've included one such example of a set of Family Fundamentals. You might consider making every Sunday night's dinnertime conversation a discussion of the Family Fundamental of the Week and how each member is going to practice it in their upcoming activities during the week. Just think of the long-term impact of focusing on one of these each week through rituals.

One of my senior consultants has even created Fundamentals for his daughter's youth basketball team. Each week, the team focuses on one of their Fundamentals so they're learning and internalizing important life lessons at the same time as working on their basketball skills. The program has been so successful with the children and their parents that it's now spread to the entire league.

Go It Alone or Get Help?

My goals in writing this book have been threefold:

1. To help you appreciate the enormous impact that the culture in any organization has on the performance of its members.
2. To help you appreciate the opportunity, and even *responsibility*, you have as a leader to intentionally create, shape, and drive the culture you want.
3. To provide you with a simple, practical, and sustainable roadmap for making that happen in your organization.

I hope by now that I've accomplished those goals, and that you're ready to embrace the opportunity that's before you. But before I send you off to begin your work, I'd like to address one remaining issue, and that's the question of whether it's better to do this work yourself or to enlist the help of outside experts.

It's an important enough question that I feel compelled to address it here, even at the considerable risk of appearing to be too "salesy." As you've seen throughout this book, I put tremendous emphasis on being practical. If it doesn't ultimately work, if it doesn't have impact, if it doesn't last, then all the theories and explanations don't really matter. And so I offer you these observations in an effort to increase your chances of success, and trust you to hear them from that perspective, and that perspective only.

Going it alone

There are three primary reasons organizations choose to do this work on their own, without the help of outside consultants. Two of those reasons are sound and responsible, while the third is rooted in a misconception.

The obvious sound reason to do this work independently, quite simply, is money. You lack the financial resources to bring in additional help. Not surprisingly, I see this most often in smaller companies. As much as they'd love to get help, they just don't have the budget to pay for it. Of course, any decision about where to allocate scarce resources is a decision about competing priorities, and one could reasonably argue that it's hard to imagine a more important priority than getting your culture right. But having said that, you may want to get working on this now and simply can't free up the money to bring in a professional. Hopefully I've provided you with enough guidance throughout this book that you can make a successful run at it.

The second reason for wanting to do this work alone is that you believe you have sufficient internal resources to drive this effort successfully, such that bringing in an outsider is simply unnecessary. I see this most often on the other end of the size spectrum. Larger companies may have entire departments devoted to change management, corporate training, workforce development, and the like. In these cases, outside help can bring an additional useful perspective, but is far less critical to success.

The third reason companies choose to go it alone is rooted in the misconception that no one knows your culture like you do, and involving a consultant in this process will cause you to lose that unique essence. While it's certainly true that you're the one who understands your culture best, a skillful consultant can help you to articulate that culture in a way that you may not have the ability to do. If they're good, they can give voice to what you want to say, and do it in a way that sounds and feels like you. Knowing your culture is not the same as being able to articulate it and drive it effectively. A good consultant can help you to do both.

Getting help

So what's the benefit of enlisting outside resources to help you in this work? Well, it's the same three reasons you choose to hire anyone to help you—time, expertise, and experience.

You and your staff undoubtedly have a plethora of initiatives you're trying to accomplish at any point in time, not to mention the everyday responsibilities of running your business! When culture work is getting "squeezed in" around everything else that's on your plate, it's destined to go through many fits and starts as competing priorities keep jumping in front of it. The committee meets to start working on the Fundamentals, but the effort to fine-tune them keeps getting pushed off because no one has the time to work on it. You've been meaning to plan that rollout but just can't seem to get to it. It's the classic struggle between working on what's urgent versus what's most important.

An external resource however, has no other objective than to help you get this done. He becomes the driving force to make sure the next call or the next meeting is scheduled. He owns the responsibility of seeing this through to completion and isn't distracted by the crush of the daily grind. Put simply, he has the time to devote to this initiative that you and your team probably don't. (Note: to be clear, an outside consultant can't *and shouldn't* entirely replace your involvement. You are critical to success. The outsider, though, can drive the process in a way that you likely can't.)

Secondly, the right consultant brings a level of expertise that you and your team probably don't possess. If I need an electrician or an attorney or a carpenter or an IT person, I get someone who's an expert in that field and ask for his or her assistance. They understand their subject matter at a level that I don't. Rather than experimenting on my own house or my business, I leverage the skills of others so that I can reap the benefit of their knowledge without having to be an expert in all things myself.

As we've discussed throughout this book, your culture is the foundation for your organization's success. It's a dangerous place to be an amateur. And if we work at it in an amateurish way, we run the risk of losing credibility if we should later try to readdress it in a more professional way.

The third reason people use professionals is for their experience. You're likely to do this process once in your leadership career. A competent professional has probably done this scores, if not hundreds of times. He's seen what works and what doesn't. He's made mistakes and learned from them. He's discovered techniques that make it more effective and realized the pitfalls that need to be avoided. You get the benefit of that wisdom without having to make the mistakes yourself. There's simply no shortcut for gaining experience.

Finding a qualified consultant

If you want to consider engaging a consultant to help you with this process, there are many resources you can turn to. While there are relatively few consultants whose practice is exclusively focused on culture, most who work in the areas of leadership coaching, strategic planning, and change management are likely to have experience in this area. Of course, in interviewing them, you'd want to understand their level of expertise as it relates specifically to culture.

With regard to finding those skilled at implementing the Fundamentals System itself, in addition to the staff of High Performing Culture who do this every day, there's a cadre of independent consultants who've been personally trained by me, have been certified in the process, and are licensed to use the tools and resources we've developed. You can find a listing of these consultants on our website (**www.highperformingculture.com**).

Regardless of which path you choose, it's not an exaggeration to say that there may not be a single initiative you could take on this year that would have as much long-term impact on the success of your organization as this one. Your culture is truly the foundation upon which everything else is built. The best time to work on it was last year. The second best time is now.

Final Thoughts

In the first chapter of this book, I noted that culture is a topic that's drawn tremendous media attention of late. Everywhere you look, from business journals to sports magazines to political editorials, people are talking about culture and its importance. And yet, as impactful as it is, surprisingly few leaders actually create their cultures intentionally.

I've tried to use this book as a way of adding to your leadership toolkit; to equip you with a simple, practical methodology for creating and driving a high-performing culture in your organization. Given just how simple and logical it is, and how transformative an impact it has, it almost begs the question, "Why don't more leaders do this?"

Beyond the reasons I noted in the second chapter, there's actually an even bigger one. Believe it or not, I think the single biggest reason that most leaders don't know what to do about their culture, assuming they understand its importance, is the *very definition of culture!* Let me explain.

When you ask most people, "What is culture?" you get a lot of vague and abstract answers. They'll say it's the "personality of a company" or it's the "environment" or it's the "collection of values and beliefs" or it's the "way things happen around here." To be sure, it *is* all of those things. The problem is that those kind of vague definitions handcuff your ability to take action. So your culture is the "personality" of your company. Try going in to work tomorrow and working on the personality of your company! What does that mean? What would you do?

Culture as behavior

If, however, we make one simple, and I think, profound paradigm shift, and we begin to see culture as *behavior*, we open up a whole world of actions we can take. In its simplest form, your culture is seen in the behavior of your people. It's what they do every day. If we change the way people behave, we change the culture.

Boiled down to its essence, the logical methodology I've presented throughout this book is nothing more than a simple behavior change model. That's really all it is. And people have been studying behavior change for centuries. Libraries are filled with volumes about behavior change. It's not all that complicated. As soon as we see culture as behavior, we equip ourselves with any number of tools and techniques that can be used to effect change. But as long as we keep describing culture in abstract, nebulous terms, what to do about it remains a mystery. That's why I'm so passionate about seeing culture through a behavior lens. It's what allows us to take action.

By chance or by design?

I'll close this book with a quote and a challenge. The quote is something I wrote years ago and it sums up the theme of this entire book. In fact, it appears on the homepage of my company's website. Here it is:

> Good companies have good cultures by chance. World-class companies have world-class cultures by design.

When I say that "good companies have good cultures by chance," I mean that if you're a good leader, you naturally tend to attract people who are mostly like you. Even if it's not an overt strategy, it happens anyway. You're like a magnet, attracting people who generally are similarly minded. As a result, I'm willing to bet you've built a pretty good team.

Further, I'll bet you treat those people reasonably well, not because you read it in a book or heard it suggested by a speaker, but because you wouldn't know how else to treat people! The core of who you are as a person and as a leader makes it difficult for you to do anything less. And as a result, you have a pretty good culture today.

My point in noting this is that you don't have to do the things I've written about here in order to be successful. After all, you've likely been pretty successful already. The formula I've outlined is *not* the difference between success and failure. Rather, it's the difference between being successful and being world-class, because that's an entirely different game.

While good companies have good cultures by chance, world-class companies are different from that. World-class companies understand just how important their culture is to the achievement of their goals, and they're simply unwilling to leave it to chance. Instead, they're incredibly purposeful, intentional, and systematic in how they author, create, and drive the culture they want. None of it is left to chance.

When I look at those individuals who truly excel, and those organizations that truly stand out, the word that best describes what makes them better than the rest is "intentionality." The good athlete has lots of talent and works hard and manages to succeed. But the world-class athlete takes that talent and hard work and is more intentional about every element of her training regimen, from how she eats, to how much she sleeps, to how she improves her skills, and even how she practices her mental game. And the same is true for organizations. Good organizations are filled with good people who work hard and care and naturally do many good things. But world-class organizations are far more intentional about everything they do—and especially about their culture.

A challenge

So, my challenge to you, as a leader, is to not allow yourself or those on your team to settle for being OK, or pretty decent, or reasonably successful. Great leadership is about helping those around you to be and do better than they ever thought they could be and do themselves. The culture you create, *by design*, is the backbone for that effort. It's what creates consistency. It's what turns greatness from being a fleeting moment of inspiration to becoming a lifelong habit.

When I speak of a "leader" here, I'm using that term in the broadest sense of the word, for we all have the opportunity to lead, and the cornerstone of this approach—clearly defining the behaviors that drive success and then creating a systematic way to teach them over and over again—is as applicable for a company as it is for a sports team or a scout troop or a family.

If you're ready to be more intentional and systematic in your approach to building (and institutionalizing) a truly high-performing culture, in whatever your leadership capacity, the 8-Step Framework provides you with the roadmap to make it happen, and the Fundamentals System™ provides you with the tools.

These simple concepts and tools have spurred a movement that's beginning to spread across the country. It's a movement of leaders who are passionate about their teams and who want to be more than good. It's a community of organizations committed to building powerful cultures and transforming themselves and their people through the continuous teaching and practice of their Fundamentals. Are you ready to join that movement? If so, welcome to the team.

David Friedman, 2018

Note from the author: As you know by now, sharing the transformative power of the Fundamentals System with as many people as possible is a deeply personal mission of mine, and I hope you'll join me in that effort by sharing this book generously. I also genuinely welcome your questions and comments. You can reach me directly at david@highperformingculture.com. Know that I personally respond to every email, and typically respond pretty darn quickly!

If you'd like to receive our bi-weekly blog, just send an email with your contact information to:

blog@highperformingculture.com.

If you'd like to receive our regular FOW message (the same one that goes to our own staff each week), just send an email with your contact information to:

FOW@highperformingculture.com.

Appendix A

Initial e-mail introducing the Fundamentals

From: David Friedman
Sent: Sunday, February 22, 2004 10:46 AM
To: All Employees
Subject: RSI Fundamental #1

By now, you've each received a copy of what I call the RSI Fundamentals. I'd like you to study these and to keep this card with you at all times. You'll notice that I've grouped the Fundamentals into four categories: Core Values, Focus on Service, The Collaborative Way, and Personal Effectiveness. These Fundamentals serve as a practical guide for our behavior; for as people, and as an organization, we *are* how we *behave*. We are not what is written on our walls and posted around the office. We are not what we talk about or even what we believe in. No, the real evidence of who we are is in the behaviors that show up on a daily basis – the behaviors that our clients, carriers, co-workers, friends, and family actually observe. We are how we behave.

Each week, we'll be featuring one of our "Fundamentals." I'll begin the week by sharing with you the text of the Fundamental as well as some thoughts and further explanation. I'll do this through both e-mail and voicemail. Additionally, I'm asking the managers to feature the week's Fundamental in departmental meetings, one-on-one meetings, and in various conversations throughout the week. I'm also asking each of you to give your own extra focus to the featured Fundamental over the course of the week. Think about what it means to you. Think about how you can demonstrate this principle even more strongly than you have in the past. Think about new ways to apply the idea in your everyday work.

Organizational (and personal) success comes from having the will and the discipline to do the basics right, day after day, week after week. Focusing on our Fundamentals is an important part of this effort, and an important part of what separates RSI from the rest.

Appendix B

In preparation for passing the baton to the management team, these were my thoughts and observations on the Fundamentals after the completion of the first 30 weeks.

From: David Friedman
Sent: Saturday, September 11, 2004 5:23 AM
To: All Employees
Subject: Thoughts and observations on the Fundamentals

As we complete the first 30 weeks of our focus on the Fundamentals, I want to let you know what's coming next, and just as importantly, I want to share some thoughts and observations with you.

As to what's next, we'll begin again by starting with Fundamental #1 and cycling through all 30 over a 30-week period. However, this time around members of our leadership team (Larry, Sharyn, Bill, Ralph, Bonnie, and Kurt) will be responsible for sending out the weekly voicemail and e-mail, adding their own thoughts on the application of the week's Fundamental. We'll also begin to institutionalize the practice of beginning any meeting at RSI with a 3-4 minute discussion of the Fundamental of the Week. This discussion can be led by any participant in the meeting, and I would encourage you to step forward and volunteer as a way of deepening your own understanding and practice of the Fundamentals.

Candidly, some might look at what we do at RSI as pretty strange! So why do we continue to focus so much effort on the Fundamentals? The answer can be found in three important concepts:

1. Cultural Alignment
2. Cultural Integrity
3. Cultural Consistency

Put simply, "cultural alignment" is when all members of the organization share common beliefs about core values and principles. I've long maintained that cultural alignment is a huge business differentiator because it leads to increased organizational speed and effectiveness. Like the scull on a river with all oarsman rowing in perfect synchronicity, an organization where all participants are working in concert has less "drag," moves more speedily, and meets challenges more effectively.

"Cultural integrity" occurs when our actions match our stated values. We may all share common beliefs and hold common points of view about guiding principles, but unless our actual behavior reflects these values, we won't all be on "the same page." Worse, a disconnect between values and behavior often leads to skepticism and cynicism, two forces that can quickly destroy the best and most well-intentioned efforts of any organization.

When our actions always match our stated values, we have "cultural consistency." People know what to expect of us simply by looking at our guiding principles. Decisions are made in the context of a philosophical framework. We ask ourselves, "What is our principle about this?" or "what do our values say we should do?"

The RSI Fundamentals are a blueprint for both our values and our behavior. By embracing them as a standard, we create cultural alignment. By putting them into everyday practice, we produce cultural integrity. By constantly teaching, deepening, and reinforcing them, we achieve cultural consistency.

While my experience tells me that this emphasis on culture is a critical element of organizational success, I must also confess that the reasons for our intense focus go deeper than that. I believe that values and principles matter in and of themselves, independent of the likely business result. I believe that working in an environment where predictable, commonly held principles guide action is inherently rewarding and, in some way, resonates inside our souls like a perfectly tuned instrument. It simply feels right on the most basic of levels, and as such, needs no business-case justification. Values and principles are like guideposts that light our way in a world that can often be confusing and difficult to navigate. Our practice of the Fundamentals is the cornerstone of this effort.

I want to thank you for helping RSI to stake out a leadership position in our industry as well as our community. We are not normal, and I'm thankful for that.

Warmly,

David

Appendix C

Sample of a CEO weekly e-mail

From: David Friedman
Sent:
To: All Employees
Subject: HPC Fundamental #7

This week's Fundamental is: **CHECK THE EGO AT THE DOOR.**

It's not about you. Don't let your ego or personal agenda get in the way of doing what's best for the team. Worrying about who gets credit or taking things personally is counterproductive. Make sure every decision is based solely on advancing company goals.

In my observation, the single biggest cause for dysfunction in organizations is ego—when people are more worried about who looks good or bad or who gets credit or blame, rather than simply focusing on making the best decisions. When we all let go of our personal agenda, and instead focus on what's best for the team, we generate a lot more success a lot faster.

As simple as it sounds, this is a Fundamental that's often misunderstood. Here are a few common examples of our ego getting in the way that we don't usually think about:

- When we take things personally, that's our ego getting in the way, thinking it's all about us.
- When we refuse to ask for help, that's our ego worrying about looking incompetent or not up to the task.
- When we hold onto a previously held belief, despite new information, that's our ego worrying about how we look when we change our mind.

- When we "defend" our idea instead of being open to other points of view, that's our ego acting as if our idea "winning" is us winning.
- When we worry more about being right rather than doing what's right, that's our ego taking over again.

Checking our ego allows for tremendous intellectual freedom because we literally focus on nothing but doing what's best for the team (or the client). We're unencumbered by any other agenda.

By the way, checking the ego at the door doesn't mean false modesty or not believing in yourself. High achievers should and do have strong, healthy egos. It means we don't make decisions to serve our ego. Here's an interesting irony about checking our ego: Those who have the strongest ego actually have the easiest time checking it at the door. Because they believe in themselves, they don't need to do things to make themselves look good. Those who have weak egos and lack confidence are usually more likely to do things to make themselves look good.

When you're about to make a decision, take a moment to notice whether you're being driven purely by what will be best, or by your own ego needs. Try letting go of your ego and watch what happens.

Warmly,

Appendix D

Tips for Fundamental of the Week e-mails

1. It's best to have the first round all come from the CEO as he/she is the Chief Cultural Officer and is the primary voice/sponsor of the culture.
2. Following the first round, it's good to have management team members cycle through the weeks, taking over authoring the weekly message. This gets additional buy-in and begins to cascade the message throughout other levels of the organization.
3. Beginning in the third round, it's very powerful to have non-management employees sign up to take on weekly messages. As you might imagine, this creates an entirely new level of ownership of the Fundamentals.
4. When writing the weekly e-mail, begin by listing the name of the Fundamental and including the description from the Fundamentals card. Then provide your own thoughts on the topic.
5. In your message, you might try to answer some of the following questions:
    a. Why is this Fundamental so important?
    b. What would it look like if everyone were doing this well?
    c. What would be the impact on the organization if everyone did this well?
    d. What would be the impact if we're not good at practicing this Fundamental?
6. It's extremely helpful to provide some stories/examples of this Fundamental in action. People remember stories and it helps them see the point more clearly.

7. The stories could be from your own experience, or perhaps an example of something you've observed in your organization. The more recent the story, the better.
8. Remember, this is your chance to teach. What do you want people to learn about this Fundamental and its importance to your success?
9. Encourage people to specifically focus on their awareness and practice of this Fundamental throughout the week. If possible, suggest some ways they might do this.
10. In terms of length, I'd recommend that your message be in the range of 2–4 paragraphs. It doesn't need to be a novel.
11. Include your message in the body of the e-mail, rather than as an attachment. This makes it more likely that people will actually read it (they don't have to take an extra step), and makes it easier for them to forward the message.
12. If you have a "group list" that includes all e-mail addresses, I would send to that list each week.
13. If some or many of your people don't have a work e-mail address, you might consider creating a company Facebook page and also posting your message there each week.
14. Try to send your e-mail at approximately the same time each week. I recommend either Sunday evening or Monday morning. This way, they start their week thinking about the Fundamental.
15. If you have a group voicemail, I encourage you to also send your message via voicemail for those who prefer to listen while they're driving or doing something else. If doing voicemail, I suggest you explain the essence of your message in a natural, conversational way, if possible, rather than simply reading your e-mail. No one really wants to listen to you read something to them.

Appendix E

Tips for starting meetings with the Fundamental of the Week

1. All scheduled meetings should begin with the Fundamental of the Week as the first agenda item.
2. The person leading the meeting should be responsible for seeing that this happens.
3. If there's a printed agenda, be sure to list this as the first agenda item.
4. Keep the discussion to no more than 3–5 minutes. If the discussion goes on too long, and begins to erode the time available for the rest of the agenda, you'll not want to continue the ritual.
5. If you're having a great conversation that you hate to stop, thank people for their engagement and suggest that anyone who can stay for a few minutes after the meeting is over is invited to continue the discussion where you left off.
6. The leader of the meeting should identify the Fundamental of the Week and then initiate the conversation.
7. The more interactive the discussion is, and the more people are involved, the better.
8. The leader may want to make a brief comment about what this Fundamental means to him/her, but then should quickly transition into getting others involved.
9. The best way to get others involved is to ask specific questions. For example,
    a. Who has a story they'd like to share where this Fundamental was relevant recently?

b. Why do you think this Fundamental is important to our success?
c. What do you think will be the impact on our company if we don't practice this Fundamental successfully?
d. What do you find to be the most challenging about practicing this Fundamental?
e. What are some of the techniques you use to practice this Fundamental?
f. What can/will you do to increase your focus on practicing this Fundamental this week?
g. How do you think you can improve how well you practice this Fundamental?

10. After you've been doing this for a while, consider asking other employees to lead a weekly discussion. Give them some advance notice so that they can feel prepared. You'll find that the level of ownership they take over the Fundamentals changes dramatically when they're asked to lead a discussion.
11. These discussions are some of your best opportunities to teach and reinforce the Fundamentals. This is where you work through the subtleties, gray areas, and nuances of them. There are many layers of nuance to these, as you'll undoubtedly see.
12. Depending on each person's role, they may be in a fair number of different meetings in a given week and will therefore talk about the week's Fundamental multiple times. That's a good thing.
13. I would encourage you to continue the practice, even in a meeting with a customer, channel partner, or vendor/supplier. It will impress them and add to their impression of you as different and better than other organizations.

Appendix F

Sample of a set of Family Fundamentals

EVANS

The Evans Family Values

1. Fill each others' bucket regularly.
2. Take responsibility. You can do and be anything. What you make of your life is up to you.
3. Your attitude is always a choice. Choose wisely.
4. Be yourself, not someone else's expectation of you.
5. Go the extra mile. Make it your best.
6. Get uncomfortable. That's how we learn.
7. Learn from your experiences. There's no such thing as failure.
8. Kindness is contagious. Go out of your way to help others.
9. Honor your commitments. Do what you say you're going to do.
10. Be flexible. Things don't always go as planned. Roll with it.
11. Be thankful. There are always those with more and those with less. Appreciate what we have.
12. Be a good listener. Learning to understand others starts with listening.
13. Laugh every day. Don't take yourself too seriously.

Acknowledgments

Writing a book is never a solo exercise, and this book was certainly no exception. A number of people played significant roles both in the production of the book itself, as well as in the development of the ideas and methodology I describe.

Sean Sweeney, a longtime friend, and co-founder of High Performing Culture, is a creative genius as well as a critical sounding board for my non-stop flow of ideas. He designed the book cover, helped with the interior layout, created our website, and makes sure they everything we produce looks first-class. It's not an exaggeration to say that this book couldn't have been completed without him.

Ruth Cohen was my extraordinary editor. Just as she did with my last book, she not only gave me valuable input on overall content and flow, but painstakingly reviewed every single sentence to be sure I expressed myself as clearly and accurately as I could. She also generously allowed me to ignore standard rules of grammar in service to letting my own natural voice come through.

Almost everything contained in this book is the result of the lessons I learned and field-tested with my original team at RSI, and more recently, with my team at High Performing Culture (HPC). Each member of my team—Sean Sweeney, Rob Wolff, Al Curnow, and Bill Kaiser—has made career sacrifices and taken on personal and financial risk to join me on this adventure. I'm indebted to them for their support, faith, and confidence, as we literally work at all times of the day and night, seven days per week, to make it all happen.

Though too numerous to mention by name, the hundreds of clients with whom we've worked have served as the true proving ground for these ideas. Their willingness to embrace the Fundamentals System, either in spite of or because of its simplicity, has enabled us to continue to fine-tune the methodology. Some of them are featured throughout the book, but there are so many others who are doing equally impressive things with their Fundamentals every day.

And last, but certainly not least, my wife Catherine has played, and continues to play, a vital role in all that I've created. Beyond serving as an extraordinary editor and proofreader for this book and all our material, she's central to the preparation of most of our products, and she boggles the mind with her willingness to serve. As most around me know, when I get focused on a project, I'm consumed almost 24/7, and that can't happen without a spouse who can manage the rest of what I'm not paying attention to. I'm fortunate indeed.

I hope you enjoyed reading *Culture by Design* as much as I enjoyed writing it.

David

Excerpt from *Fundamentally Different*

Throughout this book, I've often made reference to *Fundamentally Different* and some of its content. While my goal in *Culture by Design* has been to give you the tools to successfully create the culture you want, *Fundamentally Different* was the story of the culture we created at my first company, RSI, and specifically, the 30 Fundamentals that drove our success. Following is an excerpt from that book. I offer it as an example of the depth and teaching opportunities that are imbedded in each Fundamental.

If you'd like to read more, *Fundamentally Different* is available on Amazon in all formats: hardcover, paperback, eBook, and audio book.

FUNDAMENTAL #14

Set and ask for expectations.

We judge situations not by what happens, but by how they compare to what we expected to happen. Learn to create mutually understood expectations in every situation.

We judge situations not by what happens, but by how they compare to what we *expected* to happen. It sounds pretty simple, doesn't it? But as we take a closer look, you'll see just how big a statement it really is and why it's a cornerstone of both business and personal relationships.

Let me give you an example I often used to teach this concept to new employees at RSI. Imagine that you were a new employee coming to work for RSI and I told you at the end of the first day that one of our customs was to give each employee a check for $500 on their second morning of employment. It's just our way of saying, "We're glad to have you on board and we have confidence that you're going to be a great contributor to our organization." No doubt you'd be pretty excited and all the more certain you'd made the right choice in coming to work for us.

So now it's your second morning and on your desk when you arrive is a check for $200. You'd likely be a little disappointed. You might wonder if you'd done something wrong, or if perhaps we didn't have as much confidence in you. See, your expectation was that you'd be getting $500 and you only got $200.

Now let's try this scenario differently. Let's suppose I said nothing to you about our custom. You come in on your second day and there's a check on your desk for the very same $200. What's your reaction? You probably think you work for an amazing company (and can't wait to see what happens on the third day!).

Interestingly, the amount of money is identical in both scenarios. Yet the reaction is entirely different. So the real issue, clearly, is not the amount of the money. Rather, the issue is how reality compared to what you were expecting.

It's my observation that we have expectations for every future event. Sometimes those expectations are conscious and easily identified. We can describe them to one another. Other times, we're not as aware of our own expectations. We've never given them much thought, yet we do have expectations for everything. You have expectations for what you thought this book would be like. You have expectations for how your day at work will go. You have expectations for how a colleague will react to a message you give him. You have expectations for how your lunch will taste. You have expectations for how long a meeting will last. You literally have expectations for everything.

More importantly, your reaction to today's events will be directly related to how they compare to the expectations you had for the event—whether conscious or not. Why is this so important? Because this essential, yet obvious, principle has enormous implications for not only every service business, but for every interpersonal interaction as well.

Let's look at a typical example that happens every day in almost any business. A customer calls you on Monday morning and asks you to check on the status of their order. You promise to look into it and get back to them. The next day, proud of yourself for your responsiveness, you call with the answer. Yet the customer is unhappy that it took you so long to get back to them. They were expecting an answer the same day. Now, suppose they weren't expecting an answer until Wednesday. You're a hero because you responded by Tuesday and beat their expectation.

> *Recently, I had a situation that really showed me how important it is to ask for expectations. I had a client who was dissatisfied with the outcome of a claim issue for an employee. The client knew we took the proper steps to resolve the issue, but still wasn't satisfied. When I asked what she expected the next step to be, she revealed that she wanted us to escalate the issue through another channel at the insurance carrier, which we proceeded to do.*
>
> *Even though the final outcome ultimately wasn't the result she wanted, the client was pleased because she felt we truly advocated on their behalf. Her expectations, as we learned, were more about the lengths to which she wanted us to push than they were about whether or not the claim was going to be paid; and I would never have known this if I didn't ask.*
>
> *-Bonnie A.*

Here's the critical point to understand: If the customer is going to judge you by how your response time compares to their expectation, what could possibly be more important than finding out exactly what they're expecting? And yet we still frequently get off the phone without having established a clear expectation.

In customer service, we know that setting clear expectations for our callers is a key to ensuring satisfaction; and when we don't, we pay the price. One of our Employee Advocates (Service Representatives) was recently helping an employee who was waiting for reimbursement on a claim. The Employee Advocate asked him to complete a specific form and send it in.

A week later, the employee went to HR upset because he hadn't received the reimbursement yet, even though these claims usually take several weeks for the insurance carrier to process. Our failure to set a clear expectation for him about how long it should take for reimbursement left him guessing and, ultimately, disappointed.
-Bonnie A.

How often has someone promised to get back to you with an answer but you failed to understand when? How often have you seen sloppiness around expectations with phrases like "It shouldn't take too long" or "I'll get back to you as soon as possible?" Phrases like these are vague and increase the chances for missed expectations. My definition of "before too long" or "as soon as possible" may be very different than yours. More importantly, I'm going to judge you based upon *my* expectation, not yours.

Learn to be clear and specific in setting expectations for your own performance and in asking for expectations of others. Phrases such as "I'll get back to you by noon tomorrow" or "I'll respond before the end of business today" are clear and reduce the risk of missed expectations. It's also important to be sure that the expectations we're setting are satisfactory to our customer. For example, we might say, "I'll get back to you by Wednesday afternoon. Will that be sufficient for you?" If that doesn't work for someone, at least we're engaging in a conversation about their expectations and creating some mutually acceptable agreement.

What happens if the customer's expectation is unreasonable? By talking about expectations upfront, we have the opportunity to alter their expectation or even come up with a counterproposal that would still meet their needs. Let's suppose they say they need an answer by this afternoon, but you know it will be impossible. You might ask if getting a portion of the answer by this afternoon would still accomplish their goals with the remaining part of the answer coming by tomorrow. The key is to create agreement about the expectation. Allowing the customer to have an unrealistic expectation that goes undisclosed is a prescription for certain failure.

There's simply no reason to guess about what people expect or require of us, or what we should expect of others. Just ask!

Recovery

Are you familiar with the customer service concept known as "recovery?" This concept suggests that when a service breakdown occurs, you have an extraordinary opportunity to create loyalty. Why is this? It all has to do with understanding the role of expectations.

Let me give you an example. You and your spouse go out to dinner and have a totally satisfactory meal, with reasonable service that meets your every expectation. You're entirely contented. Who do you tell? Probably no one. Now let's suppose you go to the same restaurant and your food is served cold or is otherwise lacking. You're disappointed, and you let the manager know this. The chef comes out and personally apologizes, brings out another dish, and promises that the meal will be without charge. The manager comes over to apologize and gives you a gift certificate to return and have your next meal "on the house," and asks you to notify him directly so that he can personally see to it that your next experience is an extraordinary one. Now who do you tell? Probably lots of people. Are you likely to come back? Absolutely. So what happened here and how does it relate to expectations?

Remember that we're going to judge the event not by what happens, but by how it compares to what we're expecting to happen. In the first example, you had fairly high expectations and they were met. There was relatively little opportunity to exceed the expectations because they were already fairly high. The result was satisfaction.

In the second example, once the poor meal was served, your expectations dropped. You no longer thought as highly of the restaurant. It must have been over-rated. With the "bar" now lowered, a greater opportunity was created to exceed the expectations. As your expectations were exceeded, you became more impressed and more likely to share stories of the experience with others, and more likely to return. It's fascinating to note that the restaurant is better off having disappointed you and then recovered, than if you had not ever been disappointed in the first place. (This is not to suggest that creating disappointments is a good idea—just that disappointments create golden opportunities for exceeding expectations). "Recovery" is all about capitalizing on lowered expectations.

Here's a recovery story I remember happening in our office. One of our consultants, I'll call him Mark, was due to meet with several employees of a client to offer investment advice. The meeting was set for 7:00 am. When the client called at 7:20 to find out why Mark hadn't arrived, we became concerned. It turned out that we had an internal miscommunication about the location, and Mark had been waiting at another one of the client's sites since 6:45. By the time the error was recognized, it was too late to meet with the employees. Expectations were missed. What did we do?

Within hours, we had gotten the home addresses of the affected employees and mailed a letter of apology to each, accepting full responsibility. We included a pair of movie tickets with each letter, asking the employee to enjoy a movie on us. We then rearranged a new time to meet. The client was thrilled, and our relationship was enhanced beyond where it would have been had the error not originally happened. We exceeded the expectations.

Getting to "Unbelievable"

One of the standards we often talked about at RSI was that of being "unbelievable." We didn't want customers to be "satisfied." Rather, we wanted them to be raving about us. To understand how to achieve this, I conducted a number of focus groups among our clients over a period of years. Here's what I discovered.

Responsiveness generates excellence. Proactivity generates "unbelievable." What most customers expect is responsiveness. Give the customer what they ask for when they ask for it. In other words, meet their expectations. If you do this, they'll regard you as excellent and maybe even outstanding. However, if you want to be regarded as "unbelievable," you have to surprise them. You have to exceed their expectations. The most common way to do this is by being proactive. Offer them additional value they had not expected.

Here's a challenge we often had at RSI with regard to customer expectations—and as you read this, think about the extent to which your business probably has the same issue. We knew, of course, that customers would judge us on how we did in meeting or exceeding their expectations, yet so often we had a multitude of people who each had a hand in the setting and delivering of those expectations.

We had sales executives who made promises or commitments on behalf of the organization. We had a client who would hear and interpret those commitments and internalize them in terms of expectations. Of course, the customer's own previous history of vendor relationships also played a role in the formation of their expectations. Then, we had consultants and service professionals who were primarily responsible for the delivery of the commitments made by the sales executive and interpreted by the customer. Do you notice a problem here? With so many people part of the expectation dynamic, the situation was fraught with opportunities for misunderstanding. What I also noticed was that virtually every case of missed expectations had at its core a misunderstanding or miscommunication about what was to happen.

So, how do you solve this? It's rather simple. You make sure that all key parties understand—in writing—the primary expectations of the customer. You create an "expectations document" that outlines—in writing—all the key commitments, promises, and expectations. You make sure that the sales executive, client, consultant, and service professional all discuss and sign off on their agreement. In this way, you can be sure that the expectations are clearly understood. Then you set up a quarterly meeting with the customer to get feedback on their perception of how you're delivering on the commitments. With these pieces in place, you dramatically reduce the chance that you fall short of expectations; after all, this is how you'll be judged. I'm almost embarrassed to admit how obvious a step this is and yet we operated for so many years without it.

I've been mostly talking about expectations from a customer and vendor perspective, but the issue is identical in all human interactions. Let's see how this applies to internal relationships.

Internal Expectations

A business organization is a collection of people working together toward a common objective. It's composed of a huge number of interdependent working relationships. Sales, service, operations, administration, and finance must all be able to interact with each other successfully. Every day, hundreds, if not thousands, of conversations take place where expectations are being created. A manager asks a team member for a report. A salesperson asks for a proposal to be created. An administrator asks a teammate to get an answer.

If we fail to ask for and set expectations, we leave it entirely to chance whether we meet the expectations of another. In every conversation we have, we need to learn to discuss expectations. Ask questions like these: "By when do you need this?" "How long will that take?" "When can you have that complete?" "I need this by Thursday. Will that be possible?" "If I have this to you on Tuesday, will that work for you?"

Notice that this Fundamental says "*set* and *ask for* expectations." Both are equally important, and both parties in an interaction have an equal responsibility in expectation setting. If you're the one providing the action or the service, you need to let the other person know what to expect. How will the task be done? When? Under what conditions? At what cost? If you're on the receiving end, you need to ask for the expectations, so that you can be certain you're both on the same page.

Why We Fail to Set Expectations

Here's something I've noticed often leads to a failure to ask for expectations: Too often we confuse asking for expectations with being demanding. I watched this take place often in my years at RSI. We would call an insurance carrier on behalf of a client, and the carrier contact would promise to look into the issue and get back to us. They would not tell us when, and we too often failed to ask. Why? Because for some, it feels pushy or demanding to say, "When will you get back to me with this answer?" It feels too confrontational. Of course, you know my point of view! This is not about confrontation or about being demanding. It's about *clarity*. If we're not both working from the same set of expectations because we're too afraid to discuss them upfront, we're simply inviting misunderstanding later.

As a salesperson, I've found that an invaluable step in each and every phase of the sales process is setting and asking for expectations. From the first phone call to the close of the sale, it's so important that my prospect and I are on the "same page."

So much time is wasted on everyone's part if I don't take the time to clarify a prospect's expectations/intentions and determine mutually agreed upon expectations of what will happen next. Not doing so has resulted in, for example, several first appointments in which I prepared to go in and ask scores of questions while my prospect, however, believed that I was coming in to do a full presentation. Needless to say, neither of our expectations was met, and it was a disappointing interaction for everyone involved.

I've learned to always determine the prospect's expectations, make sure I didn't miss or misunderstand anything, and make sure we're both in sync about the next steps. Taking the time to set and ask for expectations today reduces the opportunity for misunderstandings and unfulfilled expectations tomorrow.

-Nancy N.

Another reason we often fail to ask for expectations is that it feels too awkward. I see this especially in personal situations. I recently had a call from a friend who invited me to join him and two others on a golf trip because a spot had opened up when another person had to cancel at the last minute. I was available and wanted to go, but was unsure of the expectations around who was paying for what. He hadn't set any expectations, and I felt awkward about asking. Here's a tip I've found that can help in overcoming the awkwardness: simply acknowledge the feeling to the other person, and then dive right in! I called the friend, told him that I felt a little funny asking this, but I just needed clarification about who was paying for what part of the trip. He quickly apologized for not having made it clearer, answered the question, and we were both happy. Problem solved. No misunderstanding.

Think about misunderstandings you've had with others. I'll bet virtually every one of them was related to a disconnect around expectations. Let me repeat: We judge events not by what happens, but rather by how they compare to what we expected to happen. Nothing could be more important than agreeing upon a clear set of expectations in advance.

Made in the USA
Columbia, SC
20 December 2020

29268893R00145